Christians, Unpack Your Bags!

Christians, Unpack Your Bags!

The Parable of the Weeds, the End Times, and What to Expect Before Jesus Returns

DICK LENTZ

WIPF & STOCK · Eugene, Oregon

CHRISTIANS, UNPACK YOUR BAGS!
The Parable of the Weeds, the End Times, and What to Expect Before Jesus Returns

Copyright © 2025 Dick Lentz. All rights reserved. Except for brief quotations in critical publications or reviews, no part of this book may be reproduced in any manner without prior written permission from the publisher. Write: Permissions, Wipf and Stock Publishers, 199 W. 8th Ave., Suite 3, Eugene, OR 97401.

Wipf & Stock
An Imprint of Wipf and Stock Publishers
199 W. 8th Ave., Suite 3
Eugene, OR 97401

www.wipfandstock.com

PAPERBACK ISBN: 979-8-3852-5497-2
HARDCOVER ISBN: 979-8-3852-5498-9
EBOOK ISBN: 979-8-3852-5499-6

Scripture quotations, unless otherwise noted, are taken from The Holy Bible, New International Version®, NIV®. Copyright © 1973, 1978, 1984, 2011 by Biblica, Inc.™ Used by permission of Zondervan, Hodder and Stoughton (through PLSclear), and Biblica. All rights reserved worldwide.

Scripture quotations marked GNT are taken from Good News Translation® (Today's English Version, Second Edition) © 1992 American Bible Society. All rights reserved. Used by permission.

To Janet

Then all the peoples of the earth will mourn
when they see the Son of Man coming on the clouds of heaven.
Matthew 24:30

Contents

Acknowledgments ix

Introduction xi

Chapter 1: We May Be Here for the Duration 1

Chapter 2: Two Questions 10

Chapter 3: Who Those Taken May Actually Be 24

Chapter 4: Three Things That Must Happen First 37

Chapter 5: This May Not Be Good News for Some Christians 51

Chapter 6: The Final Trumpet, Jesus' "Secret" Return, and a Bloodied Warrior 61

Chapter 7: The Three Accounts of the Return of Jesus in Revelation 76

Chapter 8: The Mark of the Beast 93

Chapter 9: Antichrists, Beasts, Tribulation, and the Last Days 107

Chapter 10: The Bride of Christ and the Pre-Wrath Rapture 118

Chapter 11: The Other Parables 128

Some Final Thoughts 135

Bibliography 139

Acknowledgments

THIS BOOK COMES FROM decades of studying and teaching the Bible, and I owe considerable thanks to those who helped bring it to fruition.

First and foremost, I want to thank my wife, Janet, who meticulously reviewed several versions of my manuscript and identified ways my writing could be improved. She was also patient when I needed to work behind closed doors to organize and write down my thoughts. Along with Janet, I want to thank my daughter, Laura, who read through some of the first iterations of my manuscript and provided valuable feedback as I endeavored to put my thoughts into readable form.

I'm grateful for the help I received from Phil and Mary Mueller, who reviewed one of my early manuscripts and provided the perspective of those less acquainted with the passages discussed in this book. I'm grateful for the input I received from my friend and mentor, Jeff Giles, as we discussed during many breakfasts some of the issues that drove me to write this book. I'm grateful for the feedback I got from my friend and co-teacher, George Koh, as we discussed over many cups of coffee some of the verses explored in this book. I am also grateful for the encouragement I received over the years from Tom Hovestol, my pastor and cheerleader.

I am especially appreciative of the members of my NEON Sunday School class, who listened throughout my thirty years of leading and teaching them. I probably learned more about God's word than they did as we studied together the passages discussed in this book.

I am deeply indebted to Katie Miller, a friend and neighbor, who did a thorough copyedit of my final manuscript. Katie corrected my grammatical errors and provided insights into how to improve the quality of this work.

Finally, I want to thank the editors I've worked with in my years of writing, including Ed Stucky at David C. Cook, and the staff and editors

Acknowledgments

at Wipf and Stock. I received valuable advice from them and others I've worked with in the publishing industry.

It is my sincere hope that this has resulted in a book whose premise is worth considering.

Introduction

I GREW UP IN a religious home. My parents were Methodists, and I learned a lot from them about what it means to have faith in God and how important it is to be obedient to him. But it wasn't until I left home and entered the Navy that I started being around Christians who said they had a personal relationship with Jesus. I saw something in them that I wanted—a peace and purpose that was different from anything I'd ever known—and, at the age of twenty, invited Jesus to dwell in my heart.

It was shortly after this that I found I had a strong desire to read and study the Bible and to share what I learned from it with others. And so, after I left the Navy, I enrolled in Simpson Bible College in San Francisco so that I could learn more about God's Word. I graduated from Simpson in 1976 with a degree in Biblical Literature and Communication.

Early in my studies at Simpson, I found myself questioning some of the more traditional interpretations of Scripture passages I heard Christians voicing. I shared this with one of my professors, and he encouraged me to look more closely at the context of passages I was questioning so that I could have a better understanding of the message the speakers or writers were trying to convey to their original audience. Over the years, I kept his advice in mind as I explored passages I had questions about, often sharing what I learned with students in the Bible studies I led.

My observation after teaching adults for over fifty years is that our understanding of Scripture is often influenced more by books we read about the Bible rather than by noting and accepting what the Bible actually says.

One of my goals when I teach and write is to provide students and readers with tools they can use to understand and interpret Scripture on their own without having to rely so heavily on outside resources. This has often resulted in them being confident they can accept Scripture at face value and believe that what the Bible says is what God meant it to say.

Introduction

Concerning the end times, many Christians believe they will be taken up to the sky to be with Jesus—that they will be "raptured"—prior to a seven-year period of extreme tribulation and judgment for those who are not followers of Jesus—those left behind. But what if this is not what Christians are destined to experience? What if the purpose of Jesus and the New Testament writers, when describing the end times, was to warn that no one will escape tribulation and that everyone, including Christians, will experience or witness nearly all the terrible events the Bible says will occur prior to the moment when Jesus returns to judge the wicked and reward the righteous?

I've concluded that this was indeed their intent. And as you read what I present in the following pages, you'll find what caused me to come to this conclusion.

But does it matter what we believe about the end times? I believe it does. For example:

- An incomplete or inaccurate understanding of what the Bible has to say about the end times can result in a faulty application of Scripture.

- We may think we are not destined to go through the period of trials typically associated with the end times. This could result in overlooking warnings in Scripture that we will be affected in some fashion by nearly all the events the Bible says will occur prior to the moment when Jesus returns to judge the wicked and reward the righteous.

- We may take our faith for granted. This could result in us not recognizing threats we are facing right now that could cause us to drift away from our faith, derail it, or deny that we know Jesus.

- We may not fully understand God's heart for the lost and the role he wants us to play in bringing them to him.

- We may not respond to the challenging times in which we live in ways that honor God.

As you read this book and look at the passages discussed, I'm confident that you'll end up with a better grasp of what the writers of Scripture wanted us to know about the end times. Hopefully this will result in a better understanding of what to expect in a world subject to all manner of difficulties, and in a desire to always be found doing what is commendable in God's eyes, no matter when Jesus returns or under what circumstances he does so.

Introduction

SOME TECHNICAL DETAILS

The following are some technical details regarding how I've presented in this book what I learned when trying to make sense of some of the end-time passages in the Bible:

- All Bible passages quoted, except as noted, come from the New International Version, 2011, translation of the Bible. I encourage readers accustomed to different translations to follow along with one they prefer, noting, as they do, both the similarities and differences in how passages are translated.

- In most chapters, I quote longer portions of passages I'm referring to in lieu of including just the verses I found significant. I did this to make it easier for readers to refer directly to the passages discussed in the text without having to flip through multiple pages of a Bible in order to do so. I also did this to provide more context for the verses emphasized in the text.

- I often use italics to highlight verses or phrases in passages I want to emphasize. This will make it easier for readers to note what I found most significant in the passages discussed.

- When the text refers to "we" or "us," it is generally referring to those who have made a personal commitment to follow Jesus or have put their trust in him for their salvation.

- When I talk about someone "being saved" or what it means "to be saved," what I'm referring to is someone whose relationship with Jesus has secured a place with him in eternity—in "heaven." What I don't mean by these phrases is being saved from the difficulties and trials of this life. What I won't discuss is how one enters into a saving relationship with Jesus. What I will point out, however, are things one must do to stay in that relationship.

- When I use the terms "the righteous" or "believers," I am referring to someone who has come into a saving relationship with Jesus. When I use the terms "the wicked," or "the unrighteous," or "unbelievers," I am referring to someone who has not entered into a saving relationship with Jesus.

- In chapter 1, I will begin discussing what the Parable of the Weeds in Matt 13:24–30 contributed to my understanding of what the Bible

Introduction

has to say about the end times and the return of Jesus. This parable is also called "the Parable of the Wheat and Weeds" and "the Parable of the Wheat and Tares." Once I introduce this parable, I will sometimes refer to it as "the Parable."

Chapter 1

We May Be Here for the Duration

The harvest is the end of the age, and the harvesters are angels.
Matthew 13:39

I'VE WONDERED FOR YEARS how the end-time events described in the Bible will unfold. For many of those years, I felt that, however they occurred, I wouldn't be around to experience them. It's not that I thought they wouldn't happen until long after I died. I believed that because I was a Christian, I was not destined to experience these terrible events and, frankly, didn't deserve to.

I thought for a long time that, though I would experience trials and troubles in this life, I would be spared from difficulties reserved for the end times, a period some call "the Great Tribulation." I concluded that I would be taken from this world prior to this time of tribulation by "the Rapture," or as some call it, "the rapture of the church." Some say the Rapture will be the moment when those who have put their faith in Jesus are taken up to the clouds to be with Jesus, and that this will be followed by a seven-year period of intense suffering and judgment for those left behind.

My belief in this was based in part on the prophecies in Dan 9. At the time Daniel was given these prophecies, the Jews had been in captivity in Babylon for seventy years. But God promised through Jeremiah that when these seventy years ended, the Israelites would be allowed to return to the land (Jer 25:11–12; 29:10–14).

In the first year of Darius the Mede's rule, Daniel recognized that these seventy years had come to an end. Daniel then "turned to God and pleaded with him in prayer and petition, in fasting, and in sackcloth and ashes" (Dan 9:3), and prayed for God to forgive the Israelites for the sins that resulted in God exiling them (Dan 9:17–19).

This is how God responded to Daniel's prayer (Dan 9:24–27):

> 24 *Seventy "sevens" are decreed for your people and your holy city to finish transgression, to put an end to sin, to atone for wickedness, to bring in everlasting righteousness, to seal up vision and prophecy and to anoint the Most Holy Place.*
>
> 25 Know and understand this: *From the time the word goes out to restore and rebuild Jerusalem until the Anointed One, the ruler, comes,* there will be *seven "sevens,"* and *sixty-two "sevens."* It will be rebuilt with streets and a trench, but in times of trouble. 26 After the sixty-two "sevens," the Anointed One will be put to death and will have nothing. The people of the ruler who will come will destroy the city and the sanctuary. The end will come like a flood: War will continue until the end, and desolations have been decreed. 27 He will confirm a covenant with many for *one "seven."* In the middle of *the "seven"* he will put an end to sacrifice and offering. And at the temple he will set up an abomination that causes desolation, until the end that is decreed is poured out on him.

The *seventy "sevens"* in this passage (v. 24) is typically understood to be 490 years (70 x 7). The *seven "sevens"* plus the *sixty-two "sevens"* (v. 25), which added together is 483 years, is the period of time beginning when "the word goes out to restore and rebuild Jerusalem" and "the Anointed One, the ruler, comes."

Some believe this 483-year period began in 458 BC when Ezra returned to Jerusalem to rebuild the temple during the reign of the Persian king Artaxerxes (Ezra 7). Others have concluded it began in 445 BC when Nehemiah was given permission by Artaxerxes to return to Jerusalem to rebuild the city's walls (Neh 2). Some think the 483 years ended with Jesus' baptism. Others contend it ended with Jesus' crucifixion.[1]

How the remaining *one "seven"* (seven years) is fulfilled is unclear (v. 27). Some believe this remaining seven years is the period of intense tribulation the world will experience following the rapture of the church—a belief in what is typically called a "pre-tribulation rapture."

There were several things that caused me to question my belief in a pre-tribulation rapture and what Christians are destined to experience as the events of the end times described in the Bible unfold. One was a

---

1. Shea, "Seventy Weeks," 135–37; Amazing Sanctuary, "2300 Days," paras. 13–14.

humbling view of myself and my own relationship with God. I realized, for example, that I wasn't much better than those I thought would be left behind when the rapture occurs. Even though I had what I considered a saving relationship with Jesus and was doing my best to live according to God's standards of righteousness, I began to question if this was enough to spare me from the terrible events that were going to occur in the end times. I wondered if I really was more deserving than non-Christians to escape from the intense period of trials the Bible says is on the horizon.

Another thing that caused me to question my beliefs regarding what I would experience in the end times was hearing how Christians experiencing persecution in third world countries often viewed it. One missionary who spent considerable time in some of these countries said that those suffering for their faith there often felt they were already living in the end times and the period the Bible calls "the great tribulation" (Rev 7:14). I concluded from this that belief in a pre-tribulation rapture was not universal among Christians and was legitimately questionable.

But perhaps the biggest reason I began to question my belief in a pre-tribulation rapture is that it took several books to make sense of it. The idea of Christians being removed from this world so they can be spared from a seven-year period of intense trials in the end times doesn't naturally jump out as one reads Scripture. It requires a handbook—or a number of them—to come to that conclusion. And what some of these books do is to connect passages in the Old Testament with passages in the New Testament that the original writers or speakers may not have intended us to connect.

The concept of a pre-tribulation rapture could be true, of course. But my doubts about it drove me to try to understand the prophecies of the end times through the ears of the original hearers, noting as I did the context in which these prophecies were given. I wanted to know who the speaker's or writer's original audience was, what issues were being addressed, and what the speaker's or writer's response to these issues was. My goal in doing this was to see if there was a better starting point for understanding prophecies of the end times than the verses in Daniel I was accustomed to using.

I found what I was looking for in the Parable of the Weeds (Matt 13:24–30):

> 24 Jesus told them another parable: "The kingdom of heaven is like a man who sowed good seed in his field. 25 But while everyone was sleeping, his enemy came and sowed weeds among the wheat,

> and went away. 26 When the wheat sprouted and formed heads, then the weeds also appeared.
>
> 27 "The owner's servants came to him and said, 'Sir, didn't you sow good seed in your field? Where then did the weeds come from?'
>
> 28 "'An enemy did this,' he replied.
>
> "The servants asked him, 'Do you want us to go and pull them up?'
>
> 29 "'No,' he answered, 'because while you are pulling the weeds, you may uproot the wheat with them. 30 Let both grow together until the harvest. At that time I will tell the harvesters: First collect the weeds and tie them in bundles to be burned; then gather the wheat and bring it into my barn.'"

The parable above is included with others in Matt 13 that focus on what the kingdom of heaven—God's kingdom—is like. At the time Jesus voiced these parables, many of the Jews who gathered to hear Jesus believed that God was going to send a messiah who would free them from the oppression of foreign rule, restore Israel's national identity, and place Israel at the head of all the nations.

Jesus spent considerable time explaining to those who followed him the actual reason he'd come to them. Jesus also described the nature of the kingdom he wanted to establish and often used parables (stories with symbolic meanings) to do so. Most who heard these stories walked away confused, however, about their actual meaning. After the crowds dispersed, Jesus sometimes explained to his most committed followers the message he was trying to convey through these stories.

This is what happened after Jesus told the above parable to those who came to hear him that day (Matt 13:36–43):

> 36 Then he left the crowd and went into the house. His disciples came to him and said, "Explain to us the parable of the weeds in the field."
>
> 37 He answered, "The one who sowed the good seed is the Son of Man. 38 The field is the world, and the good seed stands for the people of the kingdom. The weeds are the people of the evil one, 39 and the enemy who sows them is the devil. *The harvest is the end of the age*, and *the harvesters are angels*.
>
> 40 "As *the weeds are pulled up and burned in the fire*, so it will be at the end of the age. 41 The Son of Man will send out his angels, and they will weed out of his kingdom everything that causes sin and all who do evil. 42 They will throw them into the

blazing furnace, where there will be weeping and gnashing of teeth. 43 Then the righteous will shine like the sun in the kingdom of their Father. Whoever has ears, let them hear."

According to Jesus, the good seed in this parable—the wheat—are the "people of the kingdom" (v. 38). This seems to be referring to those who are faithful followers of Jesus and remain so until the *end of the age* when the *harvest takes place* (v. 39). The weeds—*the people of the evil one* (v. 38)—are those who are not followers of Jesus or are enemies of him. Note that though the servants wanted to remove the weeds from the field prior to the harvest (v. 28), the owner said this separation would not take place until the whole field was harvested (vv. 29–30). It would be at that time and not before that the weeds would be collected and burned. And it would be at that time and not before that the wheat would be harvested and brought into the barn. This meant that the wheat and the weeds were destined to be in the same field until the field was harvested.

What identifies this as an end-time passage is Jesus' statement, "The harvest is the end of the age" (v. 39). Based on this, it seems that the event this parable is referring to will not take place until Jesus returns to judge the wicked, reward the righteous, and send everyone to their eternal destination based on their relationship with him. According to this parable, this separation of the wicked from the righteous will not take place prior to the harvest—prior to the end of the age.

Jesus was addressing a misconception his disciples had regarding the relationship between the wicked and the righteous in this world. What his disciples apparently wanted was for the wicked to be taken from the world so that those left behind—those who are followers of Jesus—could live in a world free from evil. What Jesus was telling his disciples is that they were destined to live in the world alongside the unrighteous until the very last moment.

If this understanding of this parable is a valid framework for understanding the end times and what Christians can expect to experience prior to Jesus' return, then what it is telling us is that Christians will remain in this world until the end of the age and will not be rescued from it prior to the moment when Jesus returns to judge the wicked and reward the righteous.

To determine if this premise is valid, it needs to be tested to see if it is consistent with other passages in Scripture. One useful tool for doing this is a principle called "Scripture interprets Scripture." This principle is based on the observation that passages in the Bible are often interconnected. We therefore need to consider a single passage in light of the content of the verses that surround it, with an understanding of the original intent of the book or letter in which it is included, and in consideration of the Bible as a whole. We also need to look for direct connections between passages by finding those that include the same images or phrases, by identifying those that elaborate on something written or spoken about earlier, and by noting those that are in response to similar issues.

A simpler way to understand the principle of "Scripture interprets Scripture" is to remember that the first place to look when trying to understand a passage in Scripture is to Scripture itself.

I found image-matching to be a useful tool when trying to make sense of end-time passages I was questioning. "Image-matching" is the process of finding passages in the Bible that use similar images to describe an event, then using this technique to identify passages that may be describing the same event. Revelation 14:14–20, for example, includes images found in the Parable of the Weeds:

> 14 I looked, and there before me was a white cloud, and seated on the cloud was one like a son of man with a crown of gold on his head and a sharp sickle in his hand. 15 Then another angel came out of the temple and called in a loud voice to him who was sitting on the cloud, *"Take your sickle and reap, because the time to reap has come, for the harvest of the earth is ripe."* 16 So he who was seated on the cloud swung his sickle over the earth, and the earth was harvested.
>
> 17 Another angel came out of the temple in heaven, and he too had a sharp sickle. 18 Still another angel, who had charge of the fire, came from the altar and called in a loud voice to him who had the sharp sickle, "Take your sharp sickle and gather the clusters of grapes from the earth's vine, because its grapes are ripe." 19 *The angel swung his sickle* on the earth, gathered its grapes and threw them into the great winepress of God's wrath. 20 They were trampled in the winepress outside the city, and blood flowed out of the press, rising as high as the horses' bridles for a distance of 1,600 stadia.

Here are some parallels between Rev 14:14–20 and the Parable of the Weeds:

- Both describe a harvest that takes place at the end of the age (Rev 14:15; Matt 13:39).

- Both state that angels are the harvesters (Rev 14:17–19; Matt 13:39, 41).
- Both state this harvest will be a time of judgment (Rev 14:19; Matt 13:41–42).
- Both use fire to symbolize this judgment (Rev 14:18; Matt 13:42).

Based on the similarity in the images in these two passages, I've concluded they are describing the same event. Why these verses in Rev 14 are found near the middle of the book requires elaboration, something I will do in chapter 7 when I discuss the three accounts of the return of Jesus in Revelation.

Another interesting comparison between the Parable of the Weeds and other end-time passages in the Bible is where else is found the image of the wicked being thrown "into the blazing furnace, where there will be weeping and gnashing of teeth" (Matt 13:42). "Weeping and gnashing of teeth" is, for example, the fate of:

- those who are like bad fish caught in a net with good fish (Matt 13:47–50).
- those who come to a wedding banquet for a king's son without proper clothing (Matt 22:1–13).
- a servant found doing evil when his master returns from a lengthy journey (Matt 24:45–51).
- a servant who didn't invest what his master gave him while his master was away (Matt 25:28–30).

Concerning the *blazing furnace* of God's judgment, it could be the *lake of fire* recorded in Rev 20:11–15:

> 11 Then I saw a great white throne and him who was seated on it. The earth and the heavens fled from his presence, and there was no place for them. 12 And I saw the dead, great and small, standing before the throne, and books were opened. Another book was opened, which is the book of life. The dead were judged according to what they had done as recorded in the books. 13 The sea gave up the dead that were in it, and death and Hades gave up the dead that were in them, and each person was judged according to what they had done. 14 Then death and Hades were thrown into the lake of fire. The lake of fire is the second death. 15 *Anyone whose*

name was not found written in the book of life was thrown into the lake of fire.

The image of a furnace setting evildoers on fire shows up in Mal 4:1–3 as well:

> 1 "Surely the day is coming; *it will burn like a furnace*. All the arrogant and every evildoer will be stubble, and *the day that is coming will set them on fire*," says the LORD Almighty. "Not a root or a branch will be left to them. 2 But for you who revere my name, the sun of righteousness will rise with healing in its rays. And you will go out and frolic like well-fed calves. 3 Then you will trample on the wicked; *they will be ashes under the soles of your feet on the day when I act*," says the LORD Almighty.

In 2 Thess 1:6–10, the image of a blazing furnace is used to describe the day of God's judgment:

> 6 God is just: He will pay back trouble to those who trouble you 7 and give relief to you who are troubled, and to us as well. *This will happen when the Lord Jesus is revealed from heaven in blazing fire with his powerful angels.* 8 He will punish those who do not know God and do not obey the gospel of our Lord Jesus. 9 They will be punished with everlasting destruction and shut out from the presence of the Lord and from the glory of his might 10 on the day he comes to be glorified in his holy people and to be marveled at among all those who have believed. This includes you, because you believed our testimony to you.

The similarity in the images I've noted in the passages above and ones found in the Parable of the Weeds has led me to conclude that they are referring to the same event.

There are two other things I find interesting regarding what is described in 2 Thess 1:6–10. First, it mentions that "powerful angels" (v. 7) will accompany Jesus when he comes to "punish those who do not know God and do not obey the gospel of our Lord Jesus" (v. 8). This appears to be the same role angels play in the harvest described in both Rev 14:14–20 and the Parable. But 2 Thess 1:6–10 also reveals that though God promises to pay back those who trouble us (v. 6) and give relief to those who are troubled (v. 7), this will not happen until Jesus returns to punish those who have rejected him and the gospel message (v. 8).

Could it be this passage in 2 Thessalonians is reinforcing that Christians should not expect to be rescued from the trials, troubles, and tribulations of this world prior to the moment when Jesus returns to exercise judgment, and that Jesus will not return until nearly all the events described in Revelation unfold?

I've concluded this passage is indeed reinforcing this.

When I consider this, it leads me to a sobering conclusion. Although Jesus promised he will return some day to gather his followers to him, this gathering will apparently not take place until the harvest at the end of the age—until the day Jesus returns to separate the wicked from the righteous, sending each to their respective eternal destination. Until this final separation takes place, it seems we are destined to be in this world until the very end, experiencing the good and bad that is common to all, enduring along with everyone else nearly all the terrible events the Bible says will characterize the end times.

As the rest of this book unfolds, I will discuss what using the Parable of the Weeds as a framework has contributed to my understanding of other end-time passages. As I do, I will note what God wants us to do as we wait for the harvest at the end of the age.

Chapter 2

Two Questions

"Tell us," they said, "when will this happen, and what will be the sign of your coming and of the end of the age?"

MATTHEW 24:3

IN CHAPTER 1, I noted some implications if the Parable of the Weeds in Matt 13:24–30 is a valid framework for understanding passages in the Bible that describe end-time events. What this parable suggests is that followers of Jesus are destined to be in this world until the harvest at the end of the age. If this is so, then Christians can expect to witness or experience nearly all the events the Bible says will occur prior to the moment when Jesus returns to judge the wicked, reward the righteous, and send everyone to their respective eternal destination.

But if this is true—if we are destined to be in this world until the very end—what are some questions the Bible needs to answer?

Here are three I consider relevant:

- What are some challenges we will face before the end comes?
- Why will we experience these?
- How does God want us to respond when they take place?

These are questions Jesus' disciples seem to have had as well when they listened to Jesus describe the end of the age and how it was to come about. They are also questions many first-century believers likely had as

Two Questions

well, something evidenced by what writers of the New Testament had to say about the end times.

In this chapter, I will begin discussing my understanding of other passages in the Bible typically understood to be describing end-time events and how this aligns with the message Jesus seemed to have been conveying through the Parable of the Weeds. As I do this, I will provide answers to the above questions.

To begin, I'll describe the mindset Jesus' disciples seemed to have had at this point in their relationship with him. These twelve had no expectation that Jesus would be executed by Romans or that his death would provide forgiveness for sin. They thought Jesus was going to lead a revolution that would result in their nation being freed from foreign rule.[1]

They were not alone in this thinking. Most Jews shared a similar misconception about why Jesus had come to them. This is evident in how they responded when Jesus entered Jerusalem the week before he was crucified. When Jesus arrived in Jerusalem, the Jews laid palm branches at his feet (John 12:12–15). This may have signified their hope that Jesus was going to follow in the footsteps of Simon Maccabeus, who successfully established himself as king and high priest in 142 BC during a brief period of independence between Greek and Roman rule.[2]

Jesus had already told his disciples, however, that he was going to leave them (John 7:33–34):

> 33 Jesus said, "I am with you for only a short time, and then *I am going to the one who sent me.* 34 You will look for me, but you will not find me; and where I am, you cannot come."

Jesus reminded his disciples at other times that he was going away:

- 1 "Do not let your hearts be troubled. You believe in God; believe also in me. 2 My Father's house has many rooms; if that were not so, would

---

1. Acts 1:1–11 provides a good example of their mindset at that time. Following his resurrection, Jesus met with his disciples and promised they would be baptized by the Holy Spirit (v. 5). They then asked, "Lord, are you at this time going to restore the kingdom to Israel?" (v. 6). They still didn't understand, even after spending so many years with Jesus and witnessing the miracle of his resurrection, that Jesus came to establish a spiritual kingdom, not a physical one.

2. Bible Gateway, "Simon Maccabeus," 5; Brice, "Hasmonean Priest-Princes," para. 2. When Simon entered Jerusalem following his victory over the Greeks, he and his men sang "hymns of praise and thanksgiving, while carrying palm branches and playing harps, cymbals, and lyres" (1 Macc 13:51 GNT).

I have told you that *I am going there* to prepare a place for you? 3 And *if I go* and prepare a place for you, *I will come back* and take you to be with me that you also may be where I am. 4 You know the way to the place where I am going" (John 14:1–4).

- "You heard me say, '*I am going away* and *I am coming back to you.*' If you loved me, you would be glad that I am going to the Father, for the Father is greater than I" (John 14:28).

Although Jesus told his disciples that he was going away, they did not seem to understand what he meant by this or other statements about what lay ahead. They likely thought that Jesus was going on a journey, perhaps to a far-distant country, and that they would not be able to join him. Thomas, for example, responded to Jesus' statement that he was leaving them with this (John 14:5):

> Thomas said to him, "Lord, *we don't know where you are going*, so how can we know the way."

Jesus' disciples did believe that he was going to return from that journey someday, however. Jesus told them he would. And when Jesus returned, his disciples expected him to establish the kingdom he'd promised.

It is in this context that Jesus' prophecies about the end times are best understood.

I will now begin discussing my understanding of some of these prophecies, starting with Matt 24:1–30 and Luke 21:5–28, showing, as I do, how they fit the framework of the Parable of the Weeds.

THE CONTEXT

The first few verses in Matt 24:1–30 and Luke 21:5–28 provide a glimpse of some things Jesus' disciples had on their minds at that time:

- 1 Jesus left the temple and was walking away when his disciples came up to him to call his attention to its buildings. 2 "Do you see all these things?" he asked. "Truly I tell you, *not one stone here will be left on another*; every one will be thrown down."

  3 As Jesus was sitting on the Mount of Olives, the disciples came to him privately. "Tell us," they said, "*when will this happen, and what will be the sign of your coming and of the end of the age?*" (Matt 24:1–3).

- 5 Some of his disciples were remarking about how the temple was adorned with beautiful stones and with gifts dedicated to God. But Jesus said, 6 "As for what you see here, the time will come when *not one stone will be left on another*; every one of them will be thrown down."

    7 "Teacher," they asked, "*when will these things happen? And what will be the sign that they are about to take place?*" (Luke 21:5–7).

It's important to note where the event recorded took place when discussing what these verses describe. Jesus was with his disciples either near the temple in Jerusalem or on the Mount of Olives overlooking it. As they were admiring the temple, Jesus said that sometime in the future, not one stone of the temple would be left on another.

The temple they were looking at and admiring was going to be destroyed.

Jesus' disciples then asked two questions. According to Matthew, the first was, "When will this happen?" and the second, "What will be the sign of your coming and of the end of the age?" According to Luke, the first was, "When will these things happen?" and the second, "What will be the sign that they are about to take place?"

How these questions are understood affects the conclusion one draws about what events they are referring to. The mistake some seem to make in this regard is to combine the two questions into one. This sometimes results in deciding that these questions refer to the same event, and that the only thing Jesus' disciples were concerned about at that time was what would precede his return and the establishment of God's kingdom. But it's my conclusion, based on the disciples' mindset, that these questions were in regard to two separate events.

Jesus had just informed his disciples that the temple walls would one day be torn down. One thing they likely wanted to know was when the destruction of the temple was going to take place and what would indicate it was about to occur. But Jesus' disciples also wanted to know what signs would precede his return and the end of the age. Though their questions about this could be considered two questions, in context, I'm inclined to consider them one. That's because Jesus' disciples expected his return to be followed immediately by events that would result in the establishment of God's kingdom.

THE CHRONOLOGY

What follows in both Matt 24 and Luke 21 are Jesus' answers to these two questions. What makes understanding these challenging is that Matthew and Luke do not record Jesus' answers in the same order.

Here is Matthew's version (Matt 24:4–21):

> 4 Jesus answered: "Watch out that no one deceives you. 5 For many will come in my name, claiming, 'I am the Messiah,' and will deceive many. 6 You will hear of wars and rumors of wars, but see to it that you are not alarmed. Such things must happen, but the end is still to come. 7 Nation will rise against nation, and kingdom against kingdom. There will be famines and earthquakes in various places. 8 All these are the beginning of birth pains.
>
> 9 "Then you will be handed over to be persecuted and put to death, and you will be hated by all nations because of me. 10 At that time many will turn away from the faith and will betray and hate each other, 11 and many false prophets will appear and deceive many people. 12 Because of the increase of wickedness, the love of most will grow cold, 13 but the one who stands firm to the end will be saved. 14 And this gospel of the kingdom will be preached in the whole world as a testimony to all nations, and then the end will come.
>
> 15 "So when you see standing in the holy place 'the abomination that causes desolation,' spoken of through the prophet Daniel—let the reader understand— 16 then let those who are in Judea flee to the mountains. 17 Let no one on the housetop go down to take anything out of the house. 18 Let no one in the field go back to get their cloak. 19 How dreadful it will be in those days for pregnant women and nursing mothers! 20 Pray that your flight will not take place in winter or on the Sabbath. 21 For then there will be great distress, unequaled from the beginning of the world until now—and never to be equaled again."

The following summarizes Matthew's chronology of the events described:

- A time will come when many claim to be the messiah (v. 5).

- There will be wars, rumors of wars, famines, and earthquakes (vv. 6–7).

- This will not be the end, however, just mark the beginning of its birth pains (v. 6b, 8).

Two Questions

- Those who follow Jesus will be persecuted. Some will abandon their faith (vv. 9–10).
- Those who stand firm to the end will be saved (v. 13).
- The end will not come until the gospel has been preached to every nation (v. 14).
- An abomination will occur that fulfills a prophecy in Daniel regarding the destruction of the temple (v. 15).
- When this occurs, those in Judea should flee to the mountains, for what follows will be dreadful (vv. 16–21).

Here is Luke's version (Luke 21:8–24):

> 8 He replied: "Watch out that you are not deceived. For many will come in my name, claiming, 'I am he,' and, 'The time is near.' Do not follow them. 9 When you hear of wars and uprisings, do not be frightened. These things must happen first, but the end will not come right away."
>
> 10 Then he said to them: "Nation will rise against nation, and kingdom against kingdom. 11 There will be great earthquakes, famines and pestilences in various places, and fearful events and great signs from heaven.
>
> 12 *"But before all this*, they will seize you and persecute you. They will hand you over to synagogues and put you in prison, and you will be brought before kings and governors, and all on account of my name. 13 And so you will bear testimony to me. 14 But make up your mind not to worry beforehand how you will defend yourselves. 15 For I will give you words and wisdom that none of your adversaries will be able to resist or contradict. 16 You will be betrayed even by parents, brothers and sisters, relatives and friends, and they will put some of you to death. 17 Everyone will hate you because of me. 18 But not a hair of your head will perish. 19 Stand firm, and you will win life.
>
> 20 "When you see Jerusalem being surrounded by armies, you will know that its desolation is near. 21 Then let those who are in Judea flee to the mountains, let those in the city get out, and let those in the country not enter the city. 22 For this is the time of punishment in fulfillment of all that has been written. 23 How dreadful it will be in those days for pregnant women and nursing mothers! There will be great distress in the land and wrath against this people. 24 They will fall by the sword and will be taken as

prisoners to all the nations. Jerusalem will be trampled on by the Gentiles until the times of the Gentiles are fulfilled."

The following summarizes Luke's chronology:

- A day will come when many claim to be Jesus or that the end is near (v. 8).
- There will be wars, earthquakes, famines, pestilences, and other fearful events. These are not the signs of the end, however (vv. 9–11).
- "Before all this" (v. 12), those who follow Jesus will be seized, persecuted, imprisoned, and brought before kings and governors.
- This will result in opportunities to testify about Jesus (vv. 13–15).
- Some will be betrayed, and the world will hate them (vv. 16–17).
- Those who stand firm in the midst of this will win life (v. 19).
- When Jerusalem is surrounded by armies, they will know its desolation is imminent (v. 20).
- When they saw this, they should flee to the mountains, for what follows will be dreadful (vv. 21–23).
- Some will fall by the sword. Others will be taken prisoner (v. 24).
- Jerusalem will remain trampled by gentiles until the time of the gentiles is fulfilled (v. 24).

One significant difference in the two accounts is the inclusion of the phrase "But before all this" in Luke 21:12 after the description of the events described in Luke 21:8–11 (e.g., earthquakes, famines, pestilences, and other fearful things). That means that some of the events described in the verses that follow Luke 21:12 were going to occur *before* the events described in Luke 21:8–11 took place.

WHAT ACTUALLY HAPPENED

What's interesting is that nearly everything Luke 21:12–17 says would happen actually did happen to some of those listening to Jesus that day, as well as to other first-century Christians. Here are some examples:

- Some were seized (v. 12): Peter (Acts 12:3); Paul and Silas (Acts 16:19).

Two Questions

- Some were persecuted (v. 12): The apostles (Acts 5:17–18); believers in Jerusalem (Acts 8:1).
- Some were put in prison (v. 12): Peter (Acts 12:3–4); Paul (Acts 21:27, 33).
- Some spoke to kings or governors about Jesus (v. 12): Paul (Acts 24:24; 26:1).
- Some were killed (v. 16): Stephen (Acts 7:54–60); James (Acts 12:1–2).
- Some were hated because of their testimony regarding Jesus (v. 17): Stephen (Acts 7:54–60); Paul (Acts 19:23–31).

Since Luke wrote Acts as well as the Gospel that bears his name, one of his goals may have been to show in his account of the apostles' evangelistic endeavors how their efforts to do so fulfilled some of the prophecies in Luke 21 regarding what lay ahead. That doesn't mean the same things wouldn't happen to other followers of Jesus including those living today. What it does indicate is that some of these prophecies were fulfilled in the first century.

The prophecies in Matt 24 and Luke 21 regarding the destruction of the temple have likely been fulfilled as well, most likely in AD 70, in the middle of a seven-year period beginning in AD 66 and ending in AD 73.

Here is a synopsis of that period:

- AD 66: A group of Zealots in Judea revolted against the Roman authorities. In some areas, they were able to overthrow the Roman government.[3]
- AD 67: Rome responded by sending an army, commanded by Vespasian, to put down the revolt. The Romans were able to take back all of Judea and kill the remaining rebels.[4]
- A nearly two-year period of relative calm occurred as Rome responded to issues of succession following the death of Nero.[5]
- AD 70: A Roman army under Titus, son of Vespasian (who became the new emperor), besieged Jerusalem. The siege lasted seven months.[6]

---

3. Oates, "Revolt," sect. 2.
4. Oates, "Revolt," para. 16; Ludlow, "Revolt," sect. 4.
5. Ludlow, "Revolt," para. 12.
6. Oates, "Revolt," sects. 3–4.

During the siege, the daily sacrifices at the temple ceased due to lack of animals.[7]

- AD 70: Roman soldiers captured the Temple Mount. They entered the temple and desecrated its holy spots. Titus ordered that sacrifices be offered near the eastern gate of the Temple Mount. A pig was among the animals sacrificed.[8]
- AD 70: The Romans dismantled the temple, destroyed the complex, and pushed its massive stones onto the street below.[9]
- AD 70: 960 Jews took refuge on Masada, a mountain south of the Dead Sea.[10]
- AD 72: The Romans surrounded Masada. They began building a rampart so they could breach its walls.[11]
- AD 73: The Romans broke into Masada and found that most of the Jews who took refuge there had chosen death over captivity.[12]

Josephus, a first-century Jewish historian, described in his writings the extent of the suffering for those living in Jerusalem during its seven-month siege. Josephus noted that because there was no food that some resorted to eating belts and harnesses.[13] He mentioned one woman who was so hungry that she killed and ate her own child.[14]

Josephus claimed that over one million died during Jerusalem's siege[15]—by violence, disease, and starvation. Nearly one hundred thousand were taken captive and enslaved by the Romans during the four years of war.[16] Some living in or near Jerusalem at that time seemed to have heeded Jesus' advice to flee to the mountains—possibly to Masada—when they saw the Roman armies approach.

---

7. Ludlow, "Revolt," para. 14.
8. Miller, "Fall of Jerusalem," Aftermath, para. 1.
9. Ludlow, "Revolt," para. 14.
10. History, "Masada," para. 11.
11. Milligan, "Siege of Masada," paras. 5–7.
12. History, "Masada," para. 8.
13. Miller, "Fall of Jerusalem," para. 49.
14. Pareles, "Cannibal Maria," Abstract.
15. Oates, "Revolt," sect. 5.
16. Livius, "Titus' Siege," para. 22.

Two Questions

What occurred during this seven-year period is a good match for what Daniel and Jesus said was going to happen:

- Jerusalem was surrounded by an army (Luke 21:20).
- This was a dreadful time for pregnant women and nursing mothers (Matt 24:19; Luke 21:23).
- The daily sacrifices at the temple ceased (Dan 9:27).
- The Romans performed a sacrifice on the Temple Mount that was considered an abomination by the Jews (Dan 9:27; Matt 24:15).
- Some who understood the danger this posed fled to the mountains (Matt 24:16–18; Luke 21:21).
- The walls of the temple were torn down (Matt 24:1–2; Luke 21:5–6).
- Jerusalem and the temple were destroyed (Dan 9:26).
- Some Jews died by the sword. Others were taken into captivity (Luke 21:24).
- Jerusalem has been under control of gentiles (non-Jews), either wholly or in part, ever since (Luke 21:24).

Could it be that Jesus' prophecies regarding the destruction of Jerusalem and the temple have already been fulfilled? It appears that they have. If this is so, then this prophecy in Dan 9:26–27 regarding the destruction and desolation of the temple has been fulfilled as well:

> 26 After the sixty-two "sevens," the Anointed One will be put to death and will have nothing. The people of *the ruler who will come will destroy the city and the sanctuary* . . . 27 He will confirm a covenant with many for one "seven." In the middle of the "seven" he will put an *end to sacrifice and offering.* And *at the temple he will set up an abomination that causes desolation*, until the end that is decreed is poured out on him.

Matthew 24:15–16 records Jesus' association of the destruction of Jerusalem and the temple with Dan 9:26–27:

> 15 So when you see standing in the holy place *"the abomination that causes desolation," spoken of through the prophet Daniel*—let the reader understand—16 then let those who are in Judea flee to the mountains.

Was there a seven-year period in the middle of which Jerusalem was destroyed? Yes, from AD 66–73. Did the sacrifices at the temple end in the middle of this period? Yes, in AD 70, when the Jews ran out of animals that could be sacrificed, and the Romans desecrated and torched the temple. This and other events surrounding this period strongly suggest that Jesus' prophecies regarding the destruction of the temple have been fulfilled. If this is so, then no remaining portions of these prophecies or the prophecies in Dan 9 regarding the "seventy 'sevens'" (Dan 9:24), including those dangling seven years, are in our future.

Jesus may have told his disciples what events would precede the destruction of the temple so that they would know what to do when these events occurred. In the process, Jesus answered their first question, "When will this [the destruction of the temple] happen?" (Matt 24:3).

But Jesus also answered his disciples' question regarding the signs that would indicate he was about to return and that the end of the age was at hand.

WHAT IS YET TO COME

Although the history of the time suggests that some prophecies in Matt 24:1–30 and Luke 21:5–28 have already been fulfilled, there are some events described in these passages and what follows that have not. Matthew 24:22–29, for example, seems to be describing events that, for the most part, are yet to come:

> 22 If those days had not been cut short, no one would survive, but for the sake of the elect those days will be shortened. 23 At that time if anyone says to you, "Look, here is the Messiah!" or, "There he is!" do not believe it. 24 For false messiahs and false prophets will appear and perform great signs and wonders to deceive, if possible, even the elect. 25 See, I have told you ahead of time.
>
> 26 So if anyone tells you, "There he is, out in the wilderness," do not go out; or, "Here he is, in the inner rooms," do not believe it. 27 For as lightning that comes from the east is visible even in the west, so will be the coming of the Son of Man. 28 Wherever there is a carcass, there the vultures will gather.
>
> 29 Immediately after the distress of those days
> "the sun will be darkened,
>   and the moon will not give its light;
> the stars will fall from the sky,

Two Questions

and the heavenly bodies will be shaken."

This is Luke's version of the above (Luke 21:25–26):

> 25 There will be signs in the sun, moon and stars. On the earth, nations will be in anguish and perplexity at the roaring and tossing of the sea. 26 People will faint from terror, apprehensive of what is coming on the world, for the heavenly bodies will be shaken.

One of the challenges in understanding these two passages is knowing how they relate to what precedes them. The events described in Luke 21:25–26, verses that describe signs in the heavens that will result in people fainting from terror, follow the events described in Luke 21:8–11—verses that prophesy about wars, earthquakes, famines, and other fearful events that were on the horizon but did not signify the end is near. Luke then inserted between these two passages a description regarding what was going to occur in the lifetime of Jesus' disciples (Luke 21:12–24), beginning with the words, "But before all this" (v. 12), noting Jesus' warning that those who followed him were going to be persecuted and that Jerusalem was going to be destroyed. Luke then returned in verse 25 to the question of what signs would precede Jesus' return.

Understanding the sequence of events described in Matt 24:22–29 is hindered by how some translations combine verses into paragraphs. Matthew 24:22 ("*If those days* had not been cut short, no one would survive, but for the sake of the elect those days will be shortened") seems to be referring to the days surrounding the destruction of the temple, an event prophesied in Matt 24:15–21. What Jesus was telling those listening to him at that time is that if the days when Jerusalem was under siege weren't shortened, no one would survive. Matthew 24:23, which begins with "*at that time*," may then be returning to what Jesus was talking about in Matt 24:4–13—events followers of Jesus in all generations will witness or experience prior to Jesus' return. After recording Jesus' statement that the end will not come until the gospel is preached to all the nations (v. 14), Matthew described some of the signs that Jesus' return is imminent, noting, for example, the rise of false messiahs (v. 24), something Luke recorded earlier (Luke 21:8).

Both Matt 24:4–29 and Luke 21:8–26 start and end with prophecies about events that will precede Jesus' return. Both insert in between prophecies about what was going to happen to Jesus' disciples in their lifetime, along with instructions about how Jesus wanted them and others who followed him to respond when these events took place.

JESUS' RETURN

Jesus finally got around to describing what was going to happen when he returned. Here is the beginning of what Matthew recorded about this (Matt 24:30):

> Then will appear the sign of the Son of Man in heaven. And then *all the peoples of the earth will mourn when they see the Son of Man coming on the clouds of heaven*, with power and great glory.

Luke began his account of Jesus' return with this (Luke 21:27):

> At that time they will see the Son of Man coming in a cloud with power and great glory.

Both Matthew and Luke noted that, when Jesus returns, he will come in or on clouds. Both also wrote that when this happens, it will be an event visible to everyone. Neither account supports the notion of a secret gathering where followers of Jesus suddenly disappear with no understanding by those left behind of what has taken place. As Matthew noted, when Jesus returns, everyone will see him, and everyone will mourn.

In subsequent chapters, I will use the image of Jesus coming in or on clouds and the mourning that takes place when this occurs to help identify other passages in the Bible that describe the return of Jesus.

HOW THIS FITS THE FRAMEWORK

Before leaving this behind, I want to note how my understanding of Matt 24:1–30 and Luke 21:5–28 fits the framework of the Parable of the Weeds in Matt 13:24–30.

The verses below identify one explicit link between the Parable and Matthew 24:

- "The harvest is *the end of the age*, and the harvesters are angels" (Matt 13:39).
- "What will be the sign of your coming and of *the end of the age*?" (Matt 24:3).

In the Parable, Jesus told his disciples that the separation of the righteous from the unrighteous was not going to occur until the harvest at the end of the age (Matt 13:36–43). Later, Jesus' disciples asked what signs would precede his return and the end of the age (Matt 24:3). Jesus answered their question to some extent. But Jesus also described challenges they were going to face prior to his return—some things they were going to experience as they lived in the field with the "weeds"—and how they were to respond when these took place.

Jesus said that those who followed him were going to be persecuted. Some would be killed, some would be taken captive, and some would be betrayed. They would also experience wars, earthquakes, famines, and other terrifying events.

Jesus provided a clue regarding how he wanted those who followed him to respond when they faced these challenges (Matt 24:13):

> But the one who stands firm to the end will be saved.

Jesus told his disciples to stand firm in their faith, no matter what happened, and promised if they did, they would be saved.

This instruction and its associated promise are still relevant today. For if we are destined to be in the same field with the unrighteous until the end of the age, and if we are being asked as we live in this field to endure the same things Jesus told his disciples they must endure, then we will be heirs to the same promise Jesus gave to his disciples, as long as we stand firm to the end.

Jesus promised that if we remain faithful to him, no matter how difficult our circumstances may be, we will be taken into the barn along with the rest of the wheat when the harvest at the end of the age occurs.

What it means to stand firm to the end—and the consequences of not doing so—will be the topic of subsequent chapters of this book.

Chapter 3

Who Those Taken May Actually Be

> *People were eating, drinking, marrying and being given in marriage up to the day Noah entered the ark. Then the flood came and destroyed them all.*
>
> LUKE 17:27

IN THE PREVIOUS CHAPTER, I emphasized how important it is to interpret Jesus' discourse about the end times in Matthew 24:1–30 and Luke 21:5–28 in light of the two questions Jesus' disciples were asking at that time. Based on my study of these two passages, I've concluded these two questions were, "When will the temple be destroyed?" and, "What will be the signs of your return and of the end of the age?"

What comes after Matt 24:1–30 are some comparisons of Jesus' return and what follows with other real or symbolic events. In the sections below, I will note what I consider the significance of these comparisons to be and what has led me to conclude that Jesus' return will be followed by immediate, permanent, and dire consequences for those unprepared for it.

ONE IS TAKEN AND ONE IS LEFT

One thing Jesus compared his return to was what happened during the days of Noah (Matt 24:36–41):

> 36 But about that day or hour no one knows, not even the angels in heaven, nor the Son, but only the Father. 37 As it was in the days of Noah, so it will be at the coming of the Son of Man. 38 For in the

Who Those Taken May Actually Be

days before the flood, people were eating and drinking, marrying and giving in marriage, up to the day Noah entered the ark; 39 and they knew nothing about what would happen until the flood came and took them all away. That is how it will be at the coming of the Son of Man. 40 Two men will be in the field; *one will be taken and the other left*. 41 Two women will be grinding with a hand mill; *one will be taken and the other left*.

Portions of the above passage are sometimes used to support the belief that, when Jesus returns, he will remove all Christians from the face of the earth so they can be with him and will leave behind those who have not put their faith in him. Those who hold to this view typically conclude that those taken when the event described in Matt 24:36–41 takes place will be followers of Jesus. The ones who remain will be those who are not. Along with this, some believe this taking—the rapture of the church—will be followed by seven years of tribulation for those left behind. This seven-year period of trials and suffering will end when Jesus returns a second time to judge the wicked and reward the righteous.

One of the difficulties I have with the above understanding of this passage is that it requires two returns of Jesus: the first, unseen by those left behind when Jesus comes to gather his followers; the second, seven years later when Jesus returns so that he can judge each person based on their relationship with him. But as I pointed out in the previous chapter, Matt 24:30 states that Jesus' return will not be hidden from anyone. It will not be unseen. Everyone will see Jesus coming in the clouds. And this happens only once.

I also pointed out in that chapter why I've concluded that the remaining seven years in the prophecies recorded in Dan 9 were most likely fulfilled in AD 70 when the Romans destroyed Jerusalem and torched the temple.

If both of these are true—if Jesus' return will be visible to everyone, and there are no dangling seven years in Dan 9 that have to be accounted for—then the prophecies that follow Matt 24:30 are describing things that will occur after Jesus returns, an event everyone will be aware of.

But who will be taken when Jesus returns and who will be left? I find it interesting when trying to answer this question to compare Matt 24:36–41 with a similar passage in Luke 17:26–27:

26 Just as it was in the days of Noah, so also will it be in the days of the Son of Man. 27 People were eating, drinking, marrying and

being given in marriage up to the day Noah entered the ark. *Then the flood came and destroyed them all.*

Note that while Matthew said that the "flood came and *took them all away*" (Matt 24:39), Luke said that "the flood came and *destroyed them all*" (Luke 17:27). Since Luke equated being taken with being destroyed, those taken when the prophecy in Matt 24:36-41 is fulfilled will be those who are not followers of Jesus. It is those in the Parable of the Weeds that Jesus called "people of the evil one" and those "who do evil" (Matt 13:38, 41). Those left when Jesus returns will therefore be those who are followers of him. It will be those in the Parable that Jesus called "people of the kingdom" (Matt 13:38) and "the righteous" (Matt 13:43).

This understanding of what it means to be among those taken is consistent with Jesus' explanation of the Parable of the Weeds. The weeds in this parable—the unrighteous—will be removed first and will then be thrown into a blazing furnace (Matt 13:30, 40-42). What's left when this occurs will be the wheat. It will be those considered righteous.

I have also found it beneficial, when trying to make sense of who is taken in Matt 24:40-41, to note the pronouns used when describing those affected by the flood. Jesus said that, in the days before the flood, "*people were eating and drinking . . . up to the day Noah entered the ark; and they knew nothing about what would happen until the flood came and took them all away*" (Matt 24:38-39). The only "they" in these verses are the people who were eating and drinking in the days of Noah. The passage doesn't say that *he*—Noah—was taken away. It says that *they* were taken away. Although some have tried to reconcile this by observing that Noah's family also entered the ark, which could be who "they" is referring to, this insertion of Noah's family into the passage is arbitrary and not supported by the text.

I also find it interesting to note what actually happened to the people who were eating and drinking during the days of Noah (Matt 24:38; Luke 17:27). They were literally *taken away* by the waters of the flood. Just like the weeds in the Parable, they suffered grave consequences for their rejection of God and his ways.

PRINCIPLES FOR INTERPRETING PARABLES

What follows Matt 24:36-41 are five parables that describe, in symbolic language, what Jesus' return will be like, what will happen to those prepared for his return, and what will happen to those unprepared for it. These five include:

- the Parable of the Thief (Matt 24:42–44)
- the Parable of the Unfaithful Servant (Matt 24:45–51)
- the Parable of the Ten Virgins (Matt 25:1–13)
- the Parable of the Talents (Matt 25:14–30)
- the Parable of the Sheep and Goats (Matt 25:31–46)

One principle I've found useful when trying to understand parables grouped like this is to look for what they have in common and discount what they don't have in common.

Here are four characteristics I've found common in these five parables:

- Each describes *an event* that happens at an unexpected time.
- Each describes *a measure* used to decide the fate of those affected by the event.
- Each describes or implies *what happens to those unprepared* for the event.
- Each describes or implies *what happens to those prepared* for the event.

In the sections that follow, I will point out how each of these characteristics are evident in the five parables in Matt 24 and 25. I will also compare some of these parables with Luke's versions in order to clarify who they seem to be addressing.

THE PARABLE OF THE THIEF

The first parable is the Parable of the Thief (Matt 24:42–44):

> 42 Therefore keep watch, because you do not know on what day your Lord will come. 43 But understand this: If the owner of the house had known at what time of night the thief was coming, he would have kept watch and would not have let his house be broken into. 44 So you also must be ready, because the Son of Man will come at an hour when you do not expect him.

This parable compares the return of Jesus to a thief coming in the night. The following notes how it aligns with the common characteristics of the other four:

- *The event*: A thief comes in the night. No one knows when he is coming.
- *The measure*: Keeping watch; being prepared to keep the thief out.
- *Those unprepared*: House broken into. Implied: something of value is taken.
- *Those prepared*: House not broken into. Implied: nothing of value is lost.

What I find interesting is where the image of Jesus coming like a thief shows up elsewhere in Scripture. Here are three examples:

- "For you know very well that *the day of the Lord will come like a thief in the night.* 3 While people are saying, "peace and safety," destruction will come on them suddenly, as labor pains on a pregnant woman, and they will not escape" (1 Thess 5:2–3).
- "But *the day of the Lord will come like a thief.* The heavens will disappear with a roar, the elements will be destroyed by fire, and the earth and everything done in it will be laid bare" (2 Pet 3:10).
- "*Look, I come like a thief!* Blessed is the one who stays awake and remains clothed, so as not to go naked and be shamefully exposed" (Rev 16:15).

Because all three of these passages use the image of a thief to symbolize Jesus' return, it seems to me that they are describing the same event Jesus was referring to in the Parable of the Thief.

One thing that remains to be determined is who Jesus was addressing when he said his return would be like a thief coming in the night. According to Luke's version of this parable (Luke 12:35–41), it seems that Peter wondered about this as well:

> 35 "Be dressed ready for service and keep your lamps burning, 36 like servants waiting for their master to return from a wedding banquet, so that when he comes and knocks they can immediately open the door for him. 37 It will be good for those servants whose master finds them watching when he comes. Truly I tell you, he will dress himself to serve, will have them recline at the table and

will come and wait on them. 38 It will be good for those servants whose master finds them ready, even if he comes in the middle of the night or toward daybreak. 39 *But understand this: If the owner of the house had known at what hour the thief was coming, he would not have let his house be broken into.* 40 You also must be ready, because the Son of Man will come at an hour when you do not expect him."

41 Peter *asked, "Lord, are you telling this parable to us, or to everyone?"*

The following section notes how Jesus responded to Peter's question.

THE PARABLE OF THE UNFAITHFUL SERVANT

Matthew 24:45–51 describes what happens to a servant who is entrusted with his master's household and fails to do what his master demanded while his master was away:

> 45 Who then is the faithful and wise servant, whom the master has put in charge of the servants in his household to give them their food at the proper time? 46 It will be good for that servant whose master finds him doing so when he returns. 47 Truly I tell you, he will put him in charge of all his possessions. 48 But suppose that servant is wicked and says to himself, "My master is staying away a long time," 49 and he then begins to beat his fellow servants and to eat and drink with drunkards. 50 The master of that servant will come on a day when he does not expect him and at an hour he is not aware of. 51 He will cut him to pieces and assign him a place with the hypocrites, where there will be weeping and gnashing of teeth.

Here is how this parable aligns with the common characteristics of the others:

- *The event*: A master who puts a servant in charge of his household returns from a journey.
- *The measure*: How the servant treated his fellow servants while his master was away.
- *Those unprepared*: Cut to pieces. Assigned a place "where there will be weeping and gnashing of teeth."
- *Those prepared*: Put in charge of master's possessions.

This is how Luke recorded this parable (Luke 12:42–48):

> 42 *The Lord answered*, "Who then is the faithful and wise manager, whom the master puts in charge of his servants to give them their food allowance at the proper time? 43 It will be good for that servant whom the master finds doing so when he returns. 44 Truly I tell you, he will put him in charge of all his possessions. 45 But suppose the servant says to himself, 'My master is taking a long time in coming,' and he then begins to beat the other servants, both men and women, and to eat and drink and get drunk. 46 The master of that servant will come on a day when he does not expect him and at an hour he is not aware of. He will cut him to pieces and assign him a place with the unbelievers.
>
> 47 "The servant who knows the master's will and does not get ready or does not do what the master wants will be beaten with many blows. 48 But the one who does not know and does things deserving punishment will be beaten with few blows. From everyone who has been given much, much will be demanded; and from the one who has been entrusted with much, much more will be asked."

Luke's version is linked textually to Peter's question, "Lord, are you telling this parable to us, or to everyone?" (v. 41) and is Jesus' response to that question (v. 42). Jesus was confirming that terrible things will happen to unbelievers—those who do not know his will (v. 48). But worse things could happen to those who claim to be followers of Jesus if they know his will and fail to do it (v. 47).

What I find interesting about Luke 12:35–48 is that it includes images found in three of the parables recorded in Matt 24 and 25. For example, in addition to the images found in the Parable of the Unfaithful Servant (Matt 24:45–51; Luke 12:42–48):

- Luke 12:35–38 urges those waiting for their master to return from a wedding banquet to keep their lamps burning, images included in the Parable of the Ten Virgins (Matt 25:1–13), a parable I will discuss in the next section.
- Luke 12:39–40 compares a master's return to a thief breaking into a home, an image included in the Parable of the Thief (Matt 24:42–44).

These three parables in Matthew may have been combined into one discourse in Luke 12:35–48 in order to make it clear that they convey the same message. This reinforces my contention that the five parables in

Matt 24:42—25:46 should be considered as a group and not interpreted independently.

THE PARABLE OF THE TEN VIRGINS

Matthew 25 begins with a parable of ten virgins who were waiting with lamps for the coming of a bridegroom so that they could attend his wedding banquet (Matt 25:1–13):

> 1 At that time the kingdom of heaven will be like ten virgins who took their lamps and went out to meet the bridegroom. 2 Five of them were foolish and five were wise. 3 The foolish ones took their lamps but did not take any oil with them. 4 The wise ones, however, took oil in jars along with their lamps. 5 The bridegroom was a long time in coming, and they all became drowsy and fell asleep.
>
> 6 At midnight the cry rang out: "Here's the bridegroom! Come out to meet him!"
>
> 7 Then all the virgins woke up and trimmed their lamps. 8 The foolish ones said to the wise, "Give us some of your oil; our lamps are going out."
>
> 9 "No," they replied, "there may not be enough for both us and you. Instead, go to those who sell oil and buy some for yourselves."
>
> 10 But while they were on their way to buy the oil, the bridegroom arrived. The virgins who were ready went in with him to the wedding banquet. And the door was shut.
>
> 11 Later the others also came. "Lord, Lord," they said, "open the door for us!"
>
> 12 But he replied, "Truly I tell you, I don't know you."
>
> 13 Therefore keep watch, because you do not know the day or the hour.

Five of the virgins in this parable had insufficient oil to keep their lamps lit. While they were shopping for more oil, the bridegroom arrived, and he took to the wedding banquet only those virgins who had enough oil on hand to keep their lamps burning.

Here are the portions of this parable that align with the common characteristics of the others:

- *The event*: The unexpected arrival of a bridegroom who was "a long time in coming."
- *The measure*: Having enough oil so their lamps stayed lit.

- *Those unprepared*: Shut out of the wedding banquet.
- *Those prepared*: Welcomed to the wedding banquet.

I noted earlier that, when trying to understand parables grouped like this, I focus on what they have in common and discount what they don't have in common. Since this is the only parable recorded in Matt 24 and 25 that mentions a wedding, I don't consider that to be significant when trying to determine the message Jesus was conveying through this parable. In context, this parable is not describing anything that has to do with what some call "the marriage supper of the Lamb," an event described in Rev 19:6–9. The message Jesus was trying to communicate through this parable, like the others it is grouped with, is that we always need to be prepared for his return.

THE PARABLE OF THE TALENTS

Matthew 25 continues with a parable about a master who returns from a long journey and asks for an accounting from his servants of what they did with what he gave them prior to his departure (Matt 25:14–30):

> 14 Again, it will be like a man going on a journey, who called his servants and entrusted his wealth to them. 15 To one he gave five bags of gold, to another two bags, and to another one bag, each according to his ability. Then he went on his journey. 16 The man who had received five bags of gold went at once and put his money to work and gained five bags more. 17 So also, the one with two bags of gold gained two more. 18 But the man who had received one bag went off, dug a hole in the ground and hid his master's money.
>
> 19 After a long time the master of those servants returned and settled accounts with them. 20 The man who had received five bags of gold brought the other five. "Master," he said, "you entrusted me with five bags of gold. See, I have gained five more."
>
> 21 His master replied, "Well done, good and faithful servant! You have been faithful with a few things; I will put you in charge of many things. Come and share your master's happiness!"
>
> 22 The man with two bags of gold also came. "Master," he said, "you entrusted me with two bags of gold; see, I have gained two more."

Who Those Taken May Actually Be

> 23 His master replied, "Well done, good and faithful servant! You have been faithful with a few things; I will put you in charge of many things. Come and share your master's happiness!"
>
> 24 Then the man who had received one bag of gold came. "Master," he said, "I knew that you are a hard man, harvesting where you have not sown and gathering where you have not scattered seed. 25 So I was afraid and went out and hid your gold in the ground. See, here is what belongs to you."
>
> 26 His master replied, "You wicked, lazy servant! So you knew that I harvest where I have not sown and gather where I have not scattered seed? 27 Well then, you should have put my money on deposit with the bankers, so that when I returned I would have received it back with interest.
>
> 28 "'So take the bag of gold from him and give it to the one who has ten bags. 29 For whoever has will be given more, and they will have an abundance. Whoever does not have, even what they have will be taken from them. 30 And throw that worthless servant outside, into the darkness, where there will be weeping and gnashing of teeth."

Some translations of the Bible use the word "talents" to describe what this master gave to each of his servants. But a "talent," in this context, is best understood simply as a considerable sum of money.

Here are the portions of this parable that align with the common characteristics of the others:

- *The event*: A master returning from a journey asks for an accounting of what he gave his servants before he left.
- *The measure*: What they did with what he gave them.
- *Those unprepared*: Sent to a place "where there will be weeping and gnashing of teeth."
- *Those prepared*: Given more.

Like the Parable of the Ten Virgins, the details of the event described in this parable are less important than the point Jesus was trying to make. This parable is not promising that our spiritual gifts, natural abilities, or material resources will be multiplied by God if we use them wisely and for his glory. What's important is not the event described but how the message of this parable parallels the messages of the parables it is grouped with.

THE PARABLE OF THE SHEEP AND THE GOATS

The final parable in this group offers more insights about the accounting that will take place when Jesus returns (Matt 25:31–46):

> 31 When the Son of Man comes in his glory, and all the angels with him, he will sit on his glorious throne. 32 All the nations will be gathered before him, and he will separate the people one from another as a shepherd separates the sheep from the goats. 33 He will put the sheep on his right and the goats on his left.
>
> 34 Then the King will say to those on his right, "Come, you who are blessed by my Father; take your inheritance, the kingdom prepared for you since the creation of the world. 35 For I was hungry and you gave me something to eat, I was thirsty and you gave me something to drink, I was a stranger and you invited me in, 36 I needed clothes and you clothed me, I was sick and you looked after me, I was in prison and you came to visit me."
>
> 37 Then the righteous will answer him, "Lord, when did we see you hungry and feed you, or thirsty and give you something to drink? 38 When did we see you a stranger and invite you in, or needing clothes and clothe you? 39 When did we see you sick or in prison and go to visit you?"
>
> 40 The King will reply, "Truly I tell you, whatever you did for one of the least of these brothers and sisters of mine, you did for me."
>
> 41 Then he will say to those on his left, "Depart from me, you who are cursed, into the eternal fire prepared for the devil and his angels. 42 For I was hungry and you gave me nothing to eat, I was thirsty and you gave me nothing to drink, 43 I was a stranger and you did not invite me in, I needed clothes and you did not clothe me, I was sick and in prison and you did not look after me."
>
> 44 They also will answer, "Lord, when did we see you hungry or thirsty or a stranger or needing clothes or sick or in prison, and did not help you?"
>
> 45 He will reply, "Truly I tell you, whatever you did not do for one of the least of these, you did not do for me."
>
> 46 Then they will go away to eternal punishment, but the righteous to eternal life.

This is how this parable aligns with the common characteristics of the others:

- *The event*: The return of Jesus and what takes place afterwards.

- *The measure*: Doing what is commendable in God's eyes.
- *Those unprepared*: Suffer eternal punishment.
- *Those prepared*: Rewarded with eternal life.

It may seem from looking at Matt 25:31–46 that to be saved, we must literally feed the hungry, give water to the thirsty, invite strangers into our homes, give clothes to the naked, look after the sick, and visit those imprisoned (vv. 35–36). But I don't believe that Jesus' intent when telling this parable was to state that our eternal destination is determined by the degree to which we do these and other good deeds. According to the apostle Paul, we are saved by faith, not by works (Eph 2:8–9). I do believe, however, that our faith in Jesus should result in visible changes that provide evidence that our hearts are aligned with God's heart. If those changes aren't evident, when Jesus returns, we may find ourselves falling short of what is required to spend eternity with him.

James shared this same sentiment when he wrote this (Jas 2:14–17):

> 14 What good is it, my brothers and sisters, if someone claims to have faith but has no deeds? Can such faith save them? 15 Suppose a brother or a sister is without clothes and daily food. 16 If one of you says to them, "Go in peace; keep warm and well fed," but does nothing about their physical needs, what good is it? 17 In the same way, faith by itself, if it is not accompanied by action, is dead.

James was not implying that we are saved by our works. Like Jesus, James was simply saying that our faith should result in actions motivated by compassion for those in need.

CONSIDERING THEM TOGETHER

Here are some things I've concluded after considering the five parables in Matt 24 and 25 as a group, as well as passages discussed earlier:

- Jesus will return at a time when he's not expected, and this happens only once.
- There is no way to predict the day or time of Jesus' return. It is also impossible to know what conditions will precede it. We must therefore be prepared for Jesus' return at all times.

- Jesus' return will be followed by immediate, permanent, and dire consequences for those unprepared for it; however, Jesus' return will be followed by immediate, eternal, and wonderful rewards for those who are prepared for it.
- The passages discussed so far do not support a gap of time between Jesus' return and the judgment that follows. If this is so—if there is no gap of time—then there will not be a second chance after Jesus returns for those not ready for his return to repent and do what is right in his eyes.
- When Jesus returns, it will not be good to be included among those taken. It will be good, however, for those who are left.

The above is consistent with the message Jesus was trying to convey through the Parable of the Weeds. Jesus' return will be like what happens when a field is harvested. It will be the moment when the righteous and the unrighteous, who have been living together in the same field, will be separated and sent to their respective eternal destination. What the five parables in Matt 24 and 25 contribute to this is how we can be prepared for this harvest.

Chapter 4

Three Things That Must Happen First

For I tell you, you will not see me again until you say, "Blessed is he who comes in the name of the Lord."

MATTHEW 23:39

I DISCUSSED IN PREVIOUS chapters why I've concluded the Parable of the Weeds provides a legitimate framework for understanding passages in the Bible typically understood to be describing the end times. As I noted, the disciples' question—"What will be the sign of your coming and of the end of the age?" (Matt 24:3)—reveals their expectation that Jesus' return would be followed by the end of the age. This was something Jesus alluded to when he explained the meaning of the Parable and said, "The harvest is the end of the age" (Matt 13:39).

Jesus told his disciples what they were going to experience while they waited for him to return (Matt 24:9–25). They would be persecuted, some would be killed and some betrayed, and some would witness the destruction of Jerusalem and the temple within its walls. What came after this would be an extended period of time when followers of Jesus, just like wheat living alongside weeds in the same field, would experience both the good and bad events common to all.

What were they and other followers of Jesus to do as they experienced these?

They were to stand firm to the end (Matt 24:13).

Jesus explained to his disciples what lay ahead and promised he would return someday. Jesus then made this somewhat cryptic statement about what some of the events he described would signify (Matt 24:32–35):

> 32 Now learn this lesson from the fig tree: As soon as its twigs get tender and its leaves come out, you know that summer is near. 33 Even so, when you see *all these things*, you know that *it is near, right at the door*. 34 Truly I tell you, *this generation* will certainly not pass away until all these things have happened. 35 Heaven and earth will pass away, but my words will never pass away.

What Jesus didn't explain in the above passage—one some call "the Parable of the Fig Tree"—is what would be near when "all these things" occurred (v. 33). Some have concluded that Jesus was referring to the time of his return and was telling his disciples that when some of the events he spoke about earlier were occurring in increasing intensity that his return was "at the door." This has resulted in attempts to predict the timing of Jesus' return by noting the growing frequency of some of these events. But in context, it seems more likely that Jesus was simply warning his disciples once again that Jerusalem was going to be surrounded at some point by an enemy, that the temple would be desecrated (Matt 24:15), that these events would happen in their generation (Matt 24:34), and when they did, those in or near Jerusalem should flee to the mountains (Matt 24:16).

Regarding his return, Jesus said this (Matt 24:36):

> But about that day or hour no one knows, not even the angels in heaven, nor the Son, but only the Father.

The "day or hour" Jesus was referring to in the above verse was the day and hour of his return. And if Jesus has no way of knowing when or under what circumstances he will return, it is unlikely that anyone else will be able to reasonably do so.

That doesn't mean that the Bible is silent about what must take place prior to Jesus' return. Although the events described in Matt 24:4–8 (e.g., wars, rumors of war, famines, and earthquakes) have happened and will continue to do so, the Bible describes at least three events that haven't taken place but that must before Jesus returns. Because these three must occur before Jesus returns, I don't believe that Jesus will return until they do.

Here are those three:

- The Jews must acknowledge that Jesus is Lord (Matt 23:39).

- The gospel must be preached to all the nations (Matt 24:14).
- The man of lawlessness must be revealed (2 Thess 2:3).

In the sections below, I will provide my understanding of these three prophecies and how the Bible seems to indicate they will be fulfilled.

THE JEWS MUST ACKNOWLEDGE THAT JESUS IS LORD

After Jesus made his triumphal entry into Jerusalem at the beginning of the week he was crucified, he spent considerable time talking on the Temple Mount to those who came to the city to celebrate Passover. Some of Jesus' harshest words while there were reserved for teachers of the law and Pharisees who opposed him and his message (Matt 23:1–32). Jesus called them hypocrites, blind guides, and white-washed tombs (vv. 23–28). He also said this (vv. 33–34):

> 33 You snakes! You brood of vipers! How will you escape being condemned to hell? 34 Therefore I am sending you prophets and sages and teachers. Some of them you will kill and crucify; others you will flog in your synagogues and pursue from town to town.

Jesus said that these leaders—the ones who opposed him—were going to persecute the prophets and teachers he sent to them. Jesus also said they would be judged for this, and that this judgment would take place in their generation (Matt 23:35–36):

> 35 And so upon you will come all the righteous blood that has been shed on earth, from the blood of righteous Abel to the blood of Zechariah son of Berekiah, whom you murdered between the temple and the altar. 36 Truly I tell you, *all this will come on this generation.*

Jesus then said this (vv. 37–38):

> 37 Jerusalem, Jerusalem, you who kill the prophets and stone those sent to you, how often I have longed to gather your children together, as a hen gathers her chicks under her wings, and you were not willing. 38 Look, *your house is left to you desolate.*

The Jewish leaders who rejected Jesus and harbored hostility towards him and his disciples would soon find their house—the temple in Jerusalem—destroyed and left desolate.

This seems to be the event Jesus was referring to when he said this (Matt 24:15–16):

> 15 So when you see standing in the holy place *"the abomination that causes desolation,"* spoken of through the prophet Daniel—let the reader understand—16 then let those who are in Judea flee to the mountains.

It's important to note when considering this that the destruction of the temple did take place in their generation. It occurred in AD 70 when the Romans surrounded Jerusalem, tore down the walls of the temple, and destroyed it and the rest of the city.

As Jesus prophesied, their house was left to them desolate.

It is interesting in this regard to compare Jesus' statement that these leaders were going to be judged in their generation (Matt 23:36) with his warning in the Parable of the Fig Tree that "this generation will certainly not pass away until all these things have happened" (Matt 24:34). The generation Jesus was referring to in both cases appears to be their current generation, not a future one. And one thing Jesus was telling his disciples was to be found nowhere near Jerusalem when its destruction was imminent.

After Jesus prophesied that their house would be left desolate, he said this (Matt 23:39):

> For I tell you, you will not see me again until you say, "Blessed is he who comes in the name of the Lord."

Jesus said that he would not return until they—the leaders and perhaps all the Jews as well—acknowledged that he is Lord.

Jesus' statement brings to mind two questions: Does the Bible indicate what events might trigger the Jews' acknowledgment that Jesus is Lord? What happens when they do? I believe that some of the prophecies recorded in Zechariah provide answers to these questions to some extent.

Zechariah began prophesying around 520 BC during the years when the temple was being rebuilt by the Jews following its destruction by the Babylonians in 586 BC. One of God's purposes when he spoke through Zechariah was to encourage the Jews to finish rebuilding the temple in spite of the difficulties they encountered while doing so. But God also told them about a time when he was going to provide for their spiritual redemption—a time when he was going to send his "servant, the Branch" so he could "remove the sin of this land in a single day" (Zech 3:8–9). This prophecy was fulfilled when Jesus was crucified.

Three Things That Must Happen First

Zechariah 12 provides a glimpse of what was going to happen long after this. Here is how this prophecy regarding Israel's future begins (Zech 12:1–5):

> 1 A prophecy: The word of the Lord concerning Israel.
>
> The Lord, who stretches out the heavens, who lays the foundation of the earth, and who forms the human spirit within a person, declares: 2 "I am going to make Jerusalem a cup that sends all the surrounding peoples reeling. Judah will be besieged as well as Jerusalem. 3 On that day, when all the nations of the earth are gathered against her, I will make Jerusalem an immovable rock for all the nations. All who try to move it will injure themselves. 4 On that day I will strike every horse with panic and its rider with madness," declares the Lord. "I will keep a watchful eye over Judah, but I will blind all the horses of the nations. 5 Then the clans of Judah will say in their hearts, 'The people of Jerusalem are strong, because the Lord Almighty is their God.'"

Zechariah 12:1–5 describes a time when Jerusalem will be surrounded by enemies whose intent is to besiege it and Judah, the region in Israel where Jerusalem is located. Israel's enemies will not succeed, however, and will end up harming themselves when they attempt to. During this time, the Jews will recognize that their source of strength and protection is "because the Lord Almighty is their God" (v. 5).

Zechariah 12 continues by describing what else will happen at that time (Zech 12:6–9):

> 6 On that day I will make the clans of Judah like a firepot in a woodpile, like a flaming torch among sheaves. They will consume all the surrounding peoples right and left, but Jerusalem will remain intact in her place.
>
> 7 The Lord will save the dwellings of Judah first, so that the honor of the house of David and of Jerusalem's inhabitants may not be greater than that of Judah. 8 On that day the Lord will shield those who live in Jerusalem, so that the feeblest among them will be like David, and the house of David will be like God, like the angel of the Lord going before them. 9 On that day I will set out to destroy all the nations that attack Jerusalem.

Zechariah 12:6–9 indicates that God will not just give the Jews the ability to defeat their enemies. There will come a time when God intervenes directly to protect them—a time when God sets out to "destroy all the nations that attack Jerusalem" (v. 9).

This is how the Jews will respond when this takes place (Zech 12:10–14):

> 10 And I will pour out on the house of David and the inhabitants of Jerusalem a spirit of grace and supplication. *They will look on me, the one they have pierced, and they will mourn* for him as one mourns for an only child, and grieve bitterly for him as one grieves for a firstborn son. 11 On that day the weeping in Jerusalem will be as great as the weeping of Hadad Rimmon in the plain of Megiddo. 12 The land will mourn, each clan by itself, with their wives by themselves: the clan of the house of David and their wives, the clan of the house of Nathan and their wives, 13 the clan of the house of Levi and their wives, the clan of Shimei and their wives, 14 and all the rest of the clans and their wives.

Zechariah 12:10–14 describes a spiritual awakening that takes place when the Jews recognize it is God who has saved them from their enemies. It's at this point that they apparently realize that Jesus' crucifixion resulted in the death of their messiah. Jesus now, by grace, is saving them from their enemies. When this happens, they look at him and mourn.

It's also at this point that they may say, "Blessed is he who comes in the name of the Lord," something Zech 13:9 seems to confirm:

> "... I will refine them like silver
> and test them like gold.
> They will call on my name
> and I will answer them;
> I will say, 'They are my people,'
> and *they will say, 'The* Lord *is our God.'*"

It's interesting to note the emphasis in Zech 12:10–14 on the grieving, weeping, and mourning that takes place when the Jews see it is Jesus who has rescued them from their enemies. This could be part of the cacophony of mourning that takes place when "all the peoples of the earth . . . mourn when they see the Son of Man coming on the clouds of heaven" (Matt 24:30). The apostle John seems to have made this same conclusion when he included this in the opening verses of Revelation (Rev 1:7):

> "Look, *he is coming with the clouds,*"
> and "*every eye will see him,*
> *even those who pierced him*";
> and *all* peoples on earth "*will mourn* because of him."
> So shall it be! Amen.

Three Things That Must Happen First

Because Matt 24:30 states that "*all . . . will mourn* when they see the Son of Man coming on the clouds of heaven," those who mourn when Jesus returns will likely include those who are followers of Jesus as well as those who aren't. The cause of the Jews' mourning when Jesus returns could be their grief when they recognize the part they played in the death of their messiah. Christians may mourn when they recognize that there will be no more opportunities to bring family or friends into a saving relationship with Jesus. Those who have rejected Jesus and his path to salvation may mourn when they realize that it's too late for them to make a different choice regarding him.

What accompanies or follows this mourning may be what Rev 11:15–18 describes:

> 15 The seventh angel sounded his trumpet, and there were loud voices in heaven, which said:
> *"The kingdom of the world has become*
>   *the kingdom of our Lord and of his Messiah,*
>   *and he will reign for ever and ever."*
> 16 And the twenty-four elders, who were seated on their thrones before God, fell on their faces and worshiped God, 17 saying:
> "We give thanks to you, Lord God Almighty,
>   the One who is and who was,
> because you have taken your great power
>   and have begun to reign.
> 18 *The nations were angry,*
>   *and your wrath has come.*
> *The time has come for judging the dead,*
>   *and for rewarding your servants the prophets*
> *and your people who revere your name,*
>   both great and small—
> and for destroying those who destroy the earth."

What's described in Rev 11:15–18 occurs when Jesus returns to establish his kingdom (v. 15). Though no mourning is explicitly mentioned, those about to experience God's wrath will be angry, likely because of what happens next (v. 18).

The separation between those judged and those rewarded in this passage (v. 18) seems to be the same separation of the righteous from the unrighteous, symbolized by the Parable of the Weeds (Matt 13:24–30). It also seems to be the same separation and judgment described by the Parable of the Sheep and Goats (Matt 25:31–46). If this is so—if all three passages are describing the same event—then Rev 11:11–18 could be the first of three descriptions of Jesus' return in Revelation. I will discuss this in more depth in chapter 7.

THE GOSPEL MUST BE PREACHED TO ALL THE NATIONS

Matthew 24:14 records Jesus' response to his disciples' question, "What will be the sign of your coming and of the end of the age?" (Matt 24:3):

> And this gospel of the kingdom will be preached in the whole world as a testimony to all nations, and then the end will come.

According to the above verse, Jesus' return and the end of the age will not occur until the gospel has been preached to every nation.

Some believe this prophecy will be fulfilled when the Bible, or at least all of the New Testament, is translated into every language on earth. Others have concluded it will be fulfilled when the technical means for communicating the gospel is available everywhere at a single moment. Both of these interpretations of this prophecy conclude its fulfillment will come through human efforts.

There is another possibility that does not require human effort, however. Note, for example, what Rev 14:6–7 describes:

> 6 Then I saw another angel flying in midair, and *he had the eternal gospel to proclaim to those who live on the earth—to every nation, tribe, language, and people.* 7 He said in a loud voice, *"Fear God and give him glory, because the hour of his judgment has come.* Worship him who made the heavens, the earth, the sea and the springs of water."

An angel, not a human, proclaims the gospel when the above event occurs (v. 6). And this happens right before "the hour of judgment" (v. 7).

Revelation 14:14–20 describes a harvest that takes place following proclamation of the gospel by this angel:

> 14 I looked, and there before me was a *white cloud, and seated on the cloud was one like a son of man* with a crown of gold on his head and a sharp sickle in his hand. 15 Then another angel came out of the temple and called in a loud voice to him who was sitting on the cloud, "Take your sickle and reap, because the time to reap has come, *for the harvest of the earth is ripe."* 16 So he who was

seated on the cloud swung his sickle over the earth, and the earth was harvested.

17 Another angel came out of the temple in heaven, and he too had a sharp sickle. 18 Still another angel, who had charge of the fire, came from the altar and called in a loud voice to him who had the sharp sickle, "Take your sharp sickle and gather the clusters of grapes from the earth's vine, because its grapes are ripe." 19 The angel swung his sickle on the earth, gathered its grapes and threw them into the *great winepress of God's wrath*. 20 They were trampled in the winepress outside the city, and blood flowed out of the press, rising as high as the horses' bridles for a distance of 1,600 stadia.

There are several parallels between Rev 14:14–20 and end-time passages discussed earlier:

- The image of "one like the son of man" seated on "a white cloud" (v. 14) is also found in Matt 24:30, a verse that describes a time when "all the peoples of the earth . . . see the Son of Man coming on the clouds of heaven."

- This passage describes an angel coming with a sickle who harvests a crop that is ripe (vv. 17–19). This is similar to how Jesus described the harvest in the Parable of the Weeds when he said, "The harvest is the end of the age, and the harvesters are angels" (Matt 13:39).

- The judgment described (v. 19) is similar to the time of judgment Jesus warned about in the parables in Matt 24 and 25—judgment that culminates in the separation of sheep from goats—a time when "they [the unrighteous] will go away to eternal punishment, but the righteous to eternal life" (Matt 25:46).

Based on these parallels, I've concluded that Rev 14:14–20 is describing the same event Jesus was alluding to in the Parable of the Weeds as well as in the five parables recorded in Matt 24 and 25. That event is Jesus' return and the judgment that follows. If this is so, then Rev 14:14–20 could be the second of what I consider to be three descriptions of the return of Jesus in Revelation.

There are other things I find interesting about Rev 14:6–7. Note, for example, what a second angel says after proclamation of the gospel by the first angel (Rev 14:6–8):

> 6 Then I saw another angel flying in midair, and he had the eternal gospel to proclaim to those who live on the earth—to every nation, tribe, language, and people. 7 He said in a loud voice, "Fear God and give him glory, because the hour of his judgment has come. Worship him who made the heavens, the earth, the sea and the springs of water."
>
> 8 *A second angel* followed and *said,* "'*Fallen! Fallen is Babylon the Great,*' which made *all the nations drink the maddening wine of her adulteries."*

The phrases highlighted above also show up in Rev 18:1–3:

> 1 After this I saw *another angel* coming down from heaven. He had great authority, and the earth was illuminated by his splendor. 2 With a mighty voice he *shouted*:
> "'*Fallen! Fallen is Babylon the Great!*'
> She has become a dwelling for demons
> and a haunt for every impure spirit,
> a haunt for every unclean bird,
> a haunt for every unclean and detestable animal.
> 3 *For all the nations have drunk
> the maddening wine of her adulteries.*
> The kings of the earth committed adultery with her,
> and the merchants of the earth grew rich from her excessive luxuries."

In both Rev 14:8 and Rev 18:1–3, an angel proclaims that Babylon has fallen. This angel also says that all the nations have drunk "the maddening wine of her adulteries."

Some may conclude that these passages are describing two different angels proclaiming similar messages. However, I believe that they are describing the same angel proclaiming the same message. Why there are two illustrations of this event in Revelation will become clearer when I note in chapter 7 how Revelation appears to be sectioned.

I also find it interesting to note what these angels are urging people to do:

- "He said in a loud voice, '*Fear God and give him glory, because the hour of his judgment has come. Worship him* who made the heavens, the earth, the sea and the springs of water'" (Rev 14:7).
- 4 "Then I heard another voice from heaven say:

Three Things That Must Happen First

> *"'Come out of her, my people,'*
> *so that you will not share in her sins,*
> so that you will not receive any of her plagues;
> 5 for her sins are piled up to heaven,
> and God has remembered her crimes'"* (Rev 18:4–5).

Both angels are warning that a time of judgment is at hand. Both are urging people to make a choice in response to this.

As I consider the above and what these angels proclaim, it seems to me that they are warning that a time of judgment is about to come on those who are worshiping or embracing world values. But these angels are also declaring that it's not too late to repent, reject this madness, and come into a saving relationship with Jesus.

This message will be communicated to the entire world before Jesus returns, perhaps at one single moment.

This could be the event Jesus was referring to when he said, "And this gospel of the kingdom will be preached in the whole world as a testimony to all nations, and then the end will come" (Matt 24:14).

Sadly, despite these angels' efforts to urge people to repent before it's too late, many will refuse to do so:

- 20 "The rest of mankind who were not killed by these plagues still *did not repent* of the work of their hands; they did not stop worshiping demons, and idols of gold, silver, bronze, stone and wood—idols that cannot see or hear or walk. 21 *Nor did they repent* of their murders, their magic arts, their sexual immorality or their thefts" (Rev 9:20–21).

- 8 "The fourth angel poured out his bowl on the sun, and the sun was allowed to scorch people with fire. 9 They were seared by the intense heat and they cursed the name of God, who had control over these plagues, but *they refused to repent* and glorify him" (Rev 16:8–9).

- 10 "The fifth angel poured out his bowl on the throne of the beast, and its kingdom was plunged into darkness. People gnawed their tongues in agony 11 and cursed the God of heaven because of their pains and their sores, but *they refused to repent* of what they had done" (Rev 16:10–11).

Although it may seem from the above passages that efforts to preach the gospel before the final events in Revelation unfold will be futile, this conclusion would be inaccurate. Note, for example, what Rev 11:13 says will happen before the final trumpet sounds and "the kingdom of the world [becomes] the kingdom of our Lord and his Messiah":

> At that very hour there was a severe earthquake and a tenth of the city collapsed. Seven thousand people were killed in the earthquake, and *the survivors were terrified and gave glory to the God of heaven.*

I find it encouraging to know that efforts to proclaim the gospel before the end comes will bear fruit.

THE MAN OF LAWLESSNESS MUST BE REVEALED

It seems that some Christians in the first century thought that Jesus had already returned and that they had been left behind. This passage notes how the apostle Paul responded to their concerns regarding this (2 Thess 2:1–12):

> 1 Concerning the coming of our Lord Jesus Christ and our being gathered to him, we ask you, brothers and sisters, 2 not to become easily unsettled or alarmed by the teaching allegedly from us—whether by a prophecy or by word of mouth or by letter—asserting that the day of the Lord has already come. 3 Don't let anyone deceive you in any way, for *that day will not come until the rebellion occurs and the man of lawlessness is revealed, the man doomed to destruction.* 4 He will oppose and will exalt himself over everything that is called God or is worshiped, so that he sets himself up in God's temple, proclaiming himself to be God.
>
> 5 Don't you remember that when I was with you I used to tell you these things? 6 And now you know what is holding him back, so that he may be revealed at the proper time. 7 For the secret power of lawlessness is already at work; but the one who now holds it back will continue to do so till he is taken out of the way. 8 *And then the lawless one will be revealed, whom the Lord Jesus will overthrow with the breath of his mouth and destroy by the splendor of his coming.* 9 The coming of the lawless one will be in accordance with how Satan works. He will use all sorts of displays of power through signs and wonders that serve the lie, 10 and all the ways that wickedness deceives those who are perishing. They perish because they refused to love the truth and so be saved. 11 For this reason God sends them a powerful delusion so that they will believe the lie 12 and so that all will be condemned who have not believed the truth but have delighted in wickedness.

Three Things That Must Happen First

Paul said that the end of the age won't happen, and Jesus won't return, "until the rebellion occurs and the man of lawlessness is revealed" (v. 3). Paul also said that, when the lawless one is revealed, "the Lord Jesus will overthrow [him] with the breath of his mouth and destroy [him] by the splendor of his coming" (v. 8).

The prophecies noted above will likely be fulfilled when these events in Rev 19:11–21 take place:

> 11 *I saw heaven standing open and there before me was a white horse, whose rider is called Faithful and True. With justice he judges and wages war.* 12 His eyes are like blazing fire, and on his head are many crowns. He has a name written on him that no one knows but he himself. 13 He is dressed in a robe dipped in blood, and his name is the Word of God. 14 The armies of heaven were following him, riding on white horses and dressed in fine linen, white and clean. 15 *Coming out of his mouth is a sharp sword with which to strike down the nations. "He will rule them with an iron scepter."* He treads the winepress of the fury of the wrath of God Almighty. 16 On his robe and on his thigh he has this name written:
>
> KING OF KINGS AND LORD OF LORDS.
>
> 17 And I saw an angel standing in the sun, who cried in a loud voice to all the birds flying in midair, "Come, gather together for the great supper of God, 18 so that you may eat the flesh of kings, generals, and the mighty, of horses and their riders, and the flesh of all people, free and slave, great and small."
>
> 19 *Then I saw the beast and the kings of the earth and their armies gathered together to wage war against the rider on the horse and his army.* 20 But the beast was captured, and with it the false prophet who had performed the signs on its behalf. *With these signs he had deluded those who had received the mark of the beast and worshiped its image.* The two of them were thrown alive into the fiery lake of burning sulfur. 21 The rest were killed with the sword coming out of the mouth of the rider on the horse, and all the birds gorged themselves on their flesh.

Here are some parallels between 2 Thess 2:1–12 and Rev 19:11–21:

- Both events take place when Jesus returns (2 Thess 2:1; Rev 19:11).
- Both describe a rebellion led by an enemy of Jesus (2 Thess 3–4; Rev 19:19).

- Jesus' enemy is not Satan but one acting on his behalf (2 Thess 2:9; Rev 19:19–20).
- This enemy performs signs that deceive others (2 Thess 2:9; Rev 19:20).
- Jesus will overthrow and condemn this enemy (2 Thess 2:8; Rev 19:20).
- Those who follow this enemy will be condemned as well (2 Thess 2:12; Rev 19:21).

Based on these parallels, I've concluded these passages are describing the same event. I've also concluded that Rev 19:11–21 is the third of three accounts of the return of Jesus in Revelation.

WHY IT MATTERS

There are many things that Jesus said will occur before he returns. But as I've noted in this chapter, there are at least three that must occur before Jesus returns. And because they must occur, I maintain that Jesus will not return until they do occur.

It also seems that none of these three events will be preceded by signs that they are about to occur. If this is so, then it will be impossible to predict with any reasonable certainty when Jesus' return is imminent.

Chapter 5

This May Not Be Good News for Some Christians

> *Therefore keep watch, because you do not know on what day your Lord will come.*
>
> MATTHEW 24:42

As I've used the Parable of the Weeds as a framework for understanding other end-time passages, I've shown how the appearance of the same images in different end-time passages can help identify those describing the same event. In this and subsequent chapters, I will use different images but similar logic to help identify other end-time passages that may be interconnected. The first image I will do this with is the *thief* in the Parable of the Thief (Matt 24:42–44):

> 42 Therefore keep watch, because you do not know on what day your Lord will come. 43 But understand this: *If the owner of the house had known at what time of night the thief was coming, he would have kept watch* and would not have let his house be broken into. 44 So you also must be ready, because the Son of Man will come at an hour when you do not expect him.

When I discussed this parable in chapter 3, I maintained it can't be properly understood unless it is compared with the other parables in Matt 24 and 25, noting what they have in common. It was my conclusion that this parable, along with the others it is grouped with, is warning that it's imperative we always be prepared for Jesus's return, since the timing of it is unpredictable. I also noted why I've concluded that the consequences of not being prepared for Jesus' return, when he does return, will be immediate, permanent, and dire.

There are two questions I consider relevant at this point: "Who was Jesus addressing when he compared his return to a thief coming in the night?" and "What must those Jesus was addressing do to be ready for his return?" To answer these questions, I'll look at other passages that compare Jesus' return with a thief coming at a time when unexpected.

DON'T BE CAUGHT NAPPING

The comparison of Jesus' return with the coming of a thief is mentioned in two places in 1 Thess 5:1–11:

> 1 Now, brothers and sisters, about times and dates we do not need to write to you, 2 for you know very well that *the day of the Lord will come like a thief in the night.* 3 While people are saying, "Peace and safety," destruction will come on them suddenly, as labor pains on a pregnant woman, and they will not escape.
>
> 4 *But you, brothers and sisters, are not in darkness so that this day should surprise you like a thief.* 5 You are all children of the light and children of the day. We do not belong to the night or to the darkness. 6 So then, let us not be like others, who are asleep, but *let us be awake and sober.* 7 For those who sleep, sleep at night, and those who get drunk, get drunk at night. 8 But since we belong to the day, let us *be sober*, putting on faith and love as a breastplate, and the hope of salvation as a helmet. 9 *For God did not appoint us to suffer wrath* but to receive salvation through our Lord Jesus Christ. 10 He died for us so that, whether we are awake or asleep, we may live together with him. 11 Therefore *encourage one another* and *build each other up*, just as in fact you are doing.

When Paul said, "the day of the Lord will come like a thief in the night" (v. 2), it seems he was describing the same event Jesus was referring to in the Parable of the Thief. Paul also issued the same warning: Since Jesus will return at a time when he is not expected, we must be prepared for his return at all times.

Paul wrote that Jesus would return at a time when people think perhaps that the world is at peace and therefore "safe" (v. 3).

Paul also noted that Jesus' return will be followed *suddenly* by a time of destruction, from which no one will escape. It's apparent from this that there will not be a second chance for those unprepared for Jesus' return to come into a saving relationship with Jesus after he returns.

Paul pointed out that Christians, as children of the light, shouldn't be surprised by this (vv. 4–5). Unlike those who live in darkness, Christians shouldn't be caught napping (vv. 5–7). Christians should be sober minded, be people of faith and love, and be confident that their hope for salvation is in Jesus (v. 8). Christians should also continue to encourage and build up each other as they wait for Jesus to return (v. 11).

Paul was telling Christians not to live like those who have little concern about what will happen when Jesus returns, who don't believe that Jesus can return at any moment, or who think that Jesus will not return at all.

BE PREPARED

Second Peter 3:3–18 is another place where the return of Jesus is compared to the coming of a thief:

> 3 Above all, you must understand that in the last days *scoffers will come*, scoffing and following their own evil desires. 4 They will say, "Where is this 'coming' he promised? Ever since our ancestors died, everything goes on as it has since the beginning of creation." 5 But they deliberately forget that long ago by God's word the heavens came into being and the earth was formed out of water and by water. 6 By these waters also the world of that time was deluged and destroyed. 7 By the same word the present heavens and earth are reserved for fire, being kept for the day of judgment and destruction of the ungodly.
>
> 8 But do not forget this one thing, dear friends: With the Lord a day is like a thousand years, and a thousand years are like a day. 9 The Lord is not slow in keeping his promise, as some understand slowness. Instead *he is patient with you, not wanting anyone to perish*, but everyone to come to repentance.
>
> 10 *But the day of the Lord will come like a thief.* The heavens will disappear with a roar; the elements will be destroyed by fire, and the earth and everything done in it will be laid bare.
>
> 11 Since everything will be destroyed in this way, what kind of people ought you to be? You ought to *live holy and godly lives* 12 as you look forward to the day of God and speed its coming. That day will bring about the destruction of the heavens by fire, and the elements will melt in the heat. 13 But in keeping with his promise

> we are looking forward to a new heaven and a new earth, where righteousness dwells.
>
> 14 So then, dear friends, since you are looking forward to this, *make every effort to be found spotless, blameless and at peace with him*. 15 Bear in mind that our Lord's patience means salvation, just as our dear brother Paul also wrote you with the wisdom that God gave him. 16 He writes the same way in all his letters, speaking in them of these matters. His letters contain some things that are hard to understand, which ignorant and unstable people distort, as they do the other Scriptures, to their own destruction.
>
> 17 Therefore, dear friends, since you have been forewarned, *be on your guard* so that you may not be carried away by the error of the lawless and fall from your secure position. 18 But *grow in the grace and knowledge of our Lord and Savior Jesus Christ*. To him be glory both now and forever! Amen.

According to Peter, when the Day of the Lord comes, it will result in the destruction of the world we live in (v. 10). This is similar to what Paul noted when he wrote that, when Jesus returns, destruction will come suddenly upon the world (1 Thess 5:3). Similarly to what Paul wrote, there doesn't appear to be a gap of time in 2 Pet 3:3–18 between Jesus' return and the destruction that follows—no period of years for those left behind the "first time" Jesus returns to have an opportunity to get into a right relationship with Jesus before the "second time" he returns.

Peter said that some will scoff at this (vv. 3–7) and follow their own evil desires, thinking perhaps that it doesn't matter what they do, or hoping they will have a chance to repent before Jesus returns; however, Peter reminded them that though Jesus may delay his return in order to give everyone a chance to repent (v. 9), it is critical that followers of Jesus live as if he can return at any moment (vv. 10–11).

Peter elaborated on how Christians are to live in anticipation of Jesus' return. They are to "live holy and godly lives" (v. 11), make "every effort to be found spotless, blameless, and at peace with Him" (v. 14), and continue to "grow in the grace and knowledge of our Lord and Savior Jesus Christ" (v. 18).

Peter included a warning regarding what can happen if one is found unprepared when Jesus returns. After noting that some were distorting Paul's teachings regarding this (vv. 15–16), he urged believers to be on their guard, lest they get carried away by erroneous teachings and end up falling away from their secure position (v. 17).

This May Not Be Good News for Some Christians

I won't elaborate here on what it means for a Christian to fall away from their secure position. I'll save that for my discussion in chapter 8 of what the mark of the beast appears to be (Rev 13:11–18) and why I've determined it is a concern only for Christians. What I want to reinforce here is Peter's warning to always be ready for Jesus' return. We can do this by always living in ways consistent with how Jesus wants his followers to live.

WAKE UP

The *thief* shows up in two places in Revelation. The first is in Rev 3:1–6:

> 1 To the angel of the church in Sardis write: These are the words of him who holds the seven spirits of God and the seven stars. I know your deeds; you have a reputation of being alive, but *you are dead.* 2 *Wake up*! Strengthen what remains and is about to die, for *I have found your deeds unfinished* in the sight of my God. 3 *Remember*, therefore, what you have received and heard; *hold it fast*, and *repent*. But *if you do not wake up, I will come like a thief, and you will not know at what time I will come to you.*
>
> 4 Yet you have a few people in Sardis who *have not soiled their clothes*. They will walk with me, dressed in white, for they are worthy. 5 *The one who is victorious* will, like them, be dressed in white. *I will never blot out the name of that person from the book of life*, but will acknowledge that name before my Father and his angels. 6 Whoever has ears, let them hear what the Spirit says to the churches.

I find the above to be quite sobering. Jesus was addressing Christians who were part of an assembly of believers in Sardis—part of an actual church (v. 1). And they were lacking something. Jesus said they were spiritually dead (v. 1) and that their deeds were unfinished (v. 2). Jesus told them to wake up and strengthen what remained, lest what they have die (v. 2). Jesus then told them to repent (v. 3). If they didn't, Jesus said he would come like a *thief* at a time when he was unexpected (v. 3).

If Jesus came like a thief to the church at Sardis, he was going to take something of value from those who refused to heed his words.

What could potentially be taken from them? To answer that question, it's important to note what was not going to happen to those who had not "soiled their clothes" (v. 4).

According to Jesus, those who were victorious—those who had not soiled their spiritual clothes—those who exercised their faith in the ways

Jesus expects it to be exhibited—would not find their names blotted out of the book of life (v. 5). Does this mean that those in Sardis who did not exercise their faith in the ways Jesus expected it to be exercised—those who were not victorious and allowed their spiritual clothes to be soiled—could somehow find their names erased from the book of life, a book in which their names were apparently already recorded?

This passage suggests this could happen. But if it can happen, it results in a significant challenge to the belief that having one's name recorded in the book of life is permanent—and to the idea that nothing can cause God to remove it.

It's interesting to note other places in Scripture that mention the notion that someone's name can be removed from the book of life. One of these is in Exod 32 after the Israelites saw that Moses was "so long in coming down from the mountain" (v.1) and wondered what happened to him (v. 2). These verses describe Moses' response when the Israelites created an idol of gold in his absence (vv. 31–32):

> 31 So Moses went back to the LORD and said, "Oh, what a great sin these people have committed! They have made themselves gods of gold. 32 But now, please forgive their sin—but if not, then *blot me out of the book you have written.*"

Although Moses' request to have his name blotted out of "the book" may suggest that it's possible to have one's name removed from the book of life, I consider this to be a hypothetical request and simply an indication of how passionately Moses desired to have the Israelites forgiven. It seems that Moses was voicing his willingness to suffer the same fate of those who had sinned against God if God was unwilling to forgive them.

Another reference to someone's name being removed from the book of life is found in Ps 69. Although the background of this psalm is unknown, it appears that David was mired in the depths of despair and was crying out to be saved from those who hated him for no reason (vv. 1–4). David's enemies were causing him to be scorned, disgraced, and shamed (v. 19), and David asked God to do this (v. 28):

> *May they be blotted out of the book of life* and not be listed with the righteous.

David's request to have his enemies' names blotted out of the book of life seems to indicate that David thought that their names were already recorded in it. It is also evidence that he believed that their names could be removed from it. Although some might argue that what David requested is not possible, David apparently thought what he was asking for was not only possible but probable if those attacking him didn't relent.

Unlike Moses' request, David's request doesn't appear to be hypothetical.

One thing is certain: if Jesus came like a thief to the church at Sardis, it would not be good news for some of the Christians associated with it.

STAY AWAKE

Revelation 16:1–21 also includes the comparison of the return of Jesus with the coming of a thief:

> 1 Then I heard a loud voice from the temple saying to the seven angels, "Go, *pour out the seven bowls of God's wrath on the earth.*"
>
> 2 The first angel went and poured out his bowl on the land, and ugly, festering sores broke out on the people who had the mark of the beast and worshiped its image.
>
> 3 The second angel poured out his bowl on the sea, and it turned into blood like that of a dead person, and every living thing in the sea died.
>
> 4 The third angel poured out his bowl on the rivers and springs of water, and they became blood. 5 Then I heard the angel in charge of the waters say:
>
> > "You are just in these judgments, O Holy One,
> >   you who are and who were;
> > 6 for they have shed the blood of your holy people and your prophets,
> >   and you have given them blood to drink as they deserve."
> > 7 And I heard the altar respond:
> >   "Yes, Lord God Almighty,
> >   true and just are your judgments."
>
> 8 The fourth angel poured out his bowl on the sun, and the sun was allowed to scorch people with fire. 9 They were seared by the intense heat and they cursed the name of God, who had control over these plagues, but they refused to repent and glorify him.
>
> 10 The fifth angel poured out his bowl on the throne of the beast, and its kingdom was plunged into darkness. People gnawed their tongues in agony 11 and cursed the God of heaven because of their pains and their sores, but they refused to repent of what they had done.

> 12 The sixth angel poured out his bowl on the great river Euphrates, and its water was dried up to prepare the way for the kings from the East. 13 Then I saw three impure spirits that looked like frogs; they came out of the mouth of the dragon, out of the mouth of the beast and out of the mouth of the false prophet. 14 They are demonic spirits that perform signs, and they go out to the kings of the whole world, to gather them for the battle on the great day of God Almighty.
>
> 15 *"Look, I come like a thief! Blessed is the one who stays awake and remains clothed, so as not to go naked and be shamefully exposed."*
>
> 16 Then they gathered the kings together to the place that in Hebrew is called Armageddon.
>
> 17 The seventh angel poured out his bowl into the air, and out of the temple came a loud voice from the throne, saying, *"It is done!"* 18 Then there came flashes of lightning, rumblings, peals of thunder and a severe earthquake. No earthquake like it has ever occurred since mankind has been on earth, so tremendous was the quake. 19 The great city split into three parts, and the cities of the nations collapsed. God remembered Babylon the Great and gave her the cup filled with the wine of the fury of his wrath. 20 Every island fled away and the mountains could not be found. 21 From the sky huge hailstones, each weighing about a hundred pounds, fell on people. And they cursed God on account of the plague of hail, because the plague was so terrible.

I find the reference to the *thief* in verse 15 to be challenging and the most difficult to understand. It is placed in the middle of a description of seven bowls of judgment—seven instruments of God's wrath—yet doesn't appear to be placed in chronological sequence with the events described. It's as if Jesus was saying this:

> Look, I am coming, but not yet. What you need to understand is that you are going to be affected in some way by these terrible events, events that will precede my return. When these occur, stay alert, persevere, and don't lose heart. Don't give up or give in. Remain faithful, keep your spiritual clothes on, and keep those clothes clean.

The above is my understanding of Rev 16:15. And it makes sense as I consider why this mention of Jesus coming like a thief is recorded in the midst of the events described in Rev 16:1–21. It seems that though Jesus was promising that he will return, this won't happen until sometime after all the horrible events described in this passage occur—until "it is done" (v. 17). If this is so, then it's essential that we are prepared to be affected by them in some fashion, lest we find ourselves surprised or overcome by them.

This understanding of Rev 16:1–21 is consistent with my conclusion about what Jesus was telling his disciples and us in the Parable of the Weeds. For if we are destined to be in same field with unbelievers until the very last moment, then everything that happens, whether good or bad, will affect all of us in some way.

What should we do as we consider this?

We should remain faithful to Jesus no matter what circumstances we are confronted with (Matt 24:13). We should keep watch and be ready at all times for the return of Jesus (Matt 24:42–44). We should be unwavering in our faith and confident that our hope for salvation is in Jesus (1 Thess 5:8). We should live holy and godly lives (2 Pet 3:11). And if anything is found lacking within us, we should repent and strengthen what Jesus has already given us (Rev 3:2–3).

DO THE WILL OF THE LORD

Before I leave the *thief* behind, I want to return to Luke 12:35–48, a passage I mentioned in chapter 3. This passage compares Jesus' return with the return of a servant's master from a wedding banquet (v. 36), as well as to a thief coming at an hour when unexpected (v. 39). Since I quoted this passage in its entirety previously, I'm including only verses 38–40 here:

> 38 It will be good for those servants whose master finds them ready, even if he comes in the middle of the night or toward daybreak. 39 But understand this: *If the owner of the house had known at what hour the thief was coming*, he would not have let his house be broken into. 40 You also must be ready, because the Son of Man will come at an hour when you do not expect him.

As I noted earlier, after Jesus voiced the above, Peter asked, "Lord, are you telling this parable to us, or to everyone?" (Luke 12:41). Jesus responded by telling another parable: a story about an unwise servant who didn't do his master's will while his master was away (vv. 42–46). This parable concludes with this warning (vv. 47–48):

> *47 The servant who knows the master's will and does not get ready or does not do what the master wants will be beaten with many blows. 48 But the one who does not know and does things deserving punishment will be beaten with few blows. From everyone who has been given much, much will be demanded; and from the one who has been entrusted with much, much more will be asked.*

Jesus was warning that someone who knows his will and doesn't do it could suffer worse consequences than someone who doesn't know his will at all.

As I consider the implications of this, I am reminded of these two passages:

- 21 *"Not everyone who says to me, 'Lord, Lord,' will enter the kingdom of heaven, but only the one who does the will of my Father who is in heaven. 22 Many will say to me on that day, 'Lord, Lord, did we not prophesy in your name and in your name drive out demons and in your name perform many miracles?' 23 Then I will tell them plainly, 'I never knew you. Away from me, you evildoers!'"* (Matt 7:21–23).

- 14 *"What good is it, my brothers and sisters, if someone claims to have faith but has no deeds? Can such faith save them? 15 Suppose a brother or a sister is without clothes and daily food. 16 If one of you says to them, 'Go in peace; keep warm and well fed,' but does nothing about their physical needs, what good is it? 17 In the same way, faith by itself, if it is not accompanied by action, is dead"* (Jas 2:14–17).

It seems to me that if we want to spend eternity with Jesus, it isn't enough just to proclaim that Jesus is Lord. This proclamation must be followed by doing God's will—by doing what is commendable in Jesus' eyes at all times—knowing that Jesus could return at any time and ask for an accounting of what we did while he was away.

That's what I've concluded it means to be prepared for the *thief* who is coming at a time when he is unexpected. Since we don't know the day or hour Jesus will return, we have to live as if that day and hour could be at any moment.

This may not be good news for Christians who want to live as if the return of Jesus isn't imminent and they can therefore postpone doing what is right in God's eyes. For if Jesus returns at a time when he's not expected, some who claim to be followers of Jesus may suffer more extremely than those who don't know Jesus at all.

Chapter 6

The Final Trumpet, Jesus' "Secret" Return, and a Bloodied Warrior

For the trumpet will sound, the dead will be raised imperishable, and we will be changed.

1 Corinthians 15:52

In this chapter, I will continue to use image-matching to identify end-time passages that seem to be interconnected. The first image I will do this with is a trumpet sounded prior to the occurrence of a significant end-time event.

THE FINAL TRUMPET

First Corinthians 15:50–58 describes what will happen after *the last trumpet* is sounded:

> 50 I declare to you, brothers and sisters, that flesh and blood cannot inherit the kingdom of God, nor does the perishable inherit the imperishable. 51 Listen, I tell you a mystery: We will not all sleep, but *we will all be changed—* 52 *in a flash, in the twinkling of an eye, at the last trumpet. For the trumpet will sound, the dead will be raised imperishable, and we will be changed.* 53 For the perishable must clothe itself with the imperishable, and the mortal with immortality. 54 When the perishable has been clothed with the imperishable, and the mortal with immortality, then the

saying that is written will come true: "Death has been swallowed up in victory."

55 "Where, O death, is your victory?
Where, O death, is your sting?"

56 The sting of death is sin, and the power of sin is the law. 57 But thanks be to God! He gives us the victory through our Lord Jesus Christ.

58 Therefore, my dear brothers and sisters, *stand firm. Let nothing move you. Always give yourselves fully to the work of the Lord*, because you know that your labor in the Lord is not in vain.

In 1 Cor 15:1–49, Paul assured his audience that because Jesus had risen from the dead, they could be certain of a physical resurrection as well. This would result in new, imperishable bodies. This change would happen "in a flash, in the twinkling of an eye, *at the last trumpet*" (v. 52).

There are at least three points of connection between 1 Cor 15:50–58 and passages that describe the return of Jesus or other end-time events. The first is how quickly the event described takes place. It is instantaneous. And its timing appears to be unexpected. Except for the sounding of a trumpet, there doesn't seem to be even a hint that it is about to occur.

These same characteristics are found in the descriptions of Jesus' return in these verses:

- The comparison of Jesus' return to the flood in the days of Noah that those "eating and drinking . . . *knew nothing about* what would happen until the flood came and took them all away" (Matt 24:37–39).

- The comparison of Jesus' return to a *thief coming in the night* at an hour *when he is not expected* (Matt 24:42–44).

- The comparison of Jesus' return to *a master who returns* at a time when *his servant "does not expect him . . . at an hour he is not aware of"* (Matt 24:50).

- The *destruction that comes suddenly* upon those unprepared for Jesus' return (1 Thess 5:1–3).

A second point of connection between 1 Cor 15:50–58 and other end-time passages is what Paul instructed believers to do as they wait for Jesus to return. Paul urged followers of Jesus to stand firm, to not let anything move them, and to give themselves fully to the work of the Lord, knowing that their labors would not be in vain (v. 58).

The Final Trumpet, Jesus' "Secret" Return, and a Bloodied Warrior

What Paul urged followers of Jesus to do as they wait for Jesus to return is similar to what Jesus and Peter urged believers to do as well. For example:

- After Jesus described challenges his disciples and others who followed him were going to experience, he promised that those who *stand firm* to the end will be saved (Matt 24:13).

- Jesus said that only those who *do the will of the Father* will "enter the kingdom of heaven" (Matt 7:21).

- After Peter reminded Christians of the promise of "a new heaven and a new earth where righteousness dwells" (2 Pet 3:13), he urged those looking forward to that day to "*make every effort to be found spotless, blameless and at peace with him*" (2 Pet 3:14).

A third connection between 1 Cor 15:50–58 and other end-time passages is where else Scripture records a trumpet sounding in conjunction with the return of Jesus. First Thessalonians 4:13–18 is one of them:

> 13 Brothers and sisters, we do not want you to be uninformed about those who sleep in death, so that you do not grieve like the rest of mankind, who have no hope. 14 For we believe that Jesus died and rose again, and so we believe that God will bring with Jesus those who have fallen asleep in him. 15 According to the Lord's word, we tell you that we who are still alive, who are left until the coming of the Lord, will certainly not precede those who have fallen asleep. 16 *For the Lord himself will come down from heaven, with a loud command, with the voice of the archangel and with the trumpet call of God, and the dead in Christ will rise first.* 17 After that, we who are still alive and are left will be caught up together with them in the clouds to meet the Lord in the air. And so we will be with the Lord forever. 18 Therefore *encourage one another* with these words.

First Thessalonians 4:13–18 has at least three points of connection with 1 Cor 15:50–58. For example, in addition to noting that Jesus' return will be announced by a trumpet call (1 Thess 4:16; 1 Cor 15:52),

- It emphasizes the promise that followers of Jesus will be resurrected from the dead when Jesus returns (1 Thess 4:16; 1 Cor 15:52).

- It urges those who follow Jesus to let this promise be a source of encouragement (1 Thess 4:18; 1 Cor 15:58).

Matthew 24:30-31 also states that Jesus' return will be announced by a trumpet call:

> 30 Then will appear the sign of the Son of Man in heaven. And then all the peoples of the earth will mourn when they see the Son of Man coming on the clouds of heaven, with power and great glory. 31 And *he will send his angels with a loud trumpet call, and they will gather his elect* from the four winds, from one end of the heavens to the other.

The gathering described in Matt 24:31—one that occurs when Jesus returns, and one accompanied by "a loud trumpet call"—seems to be the same gathering described in 1 Cor 15:52 when "the dead will be raised imperishable," an event accompanied by a sounding trumpet as well.

There is a connection between 1 Cor 15:50-58 and Revelation that I consider even more significant. Note Paul's statement in 1 Cor 15:52 that the event described—the return of Jesus and, along with that, the resurrection of the dead—will occur "at the *last* trumpet." This implies that there will be multiple trumpets that sound prior to the return of Jesus.

Is there any place in Scripture where a sequence of sounding trumpets precedes a number of end-time events?

There is, beginning with the description of the breaking of the seventh seal in Rev 8:1-2:

> 1 When he opened the seventh seal, there was silence in heaven for about half an hour.
> 2 And *I saw the seven angels* who stand before God, and *seven trumpets were given to them.*

Each of the first six angels in the above blows a trumpet before the occurrence of a significant end-time event. Revelation 8:6—9:19 describes these events. Each is more challenging or destructive than the ones described earlier.

This is what Rev 11:15-18 says will happen when the seventh angel sounds his trumpet:

> 15 *The seventh angel sounded his trumpet,* and there were loud voices in heaven, which said:
> "The kingdom of the world has become
>   the kingdom of our Lord and of his Messiah,
>   and he will reign for ever and ever."
> 16 And the twenty-four elders, who were seated on their thrones before God, fell on their faces and worshiped God, 17 saying:

> "We give thanks to you, Lord God Almighty,
>   the One who is and who was,
> because you have taken your great power
>   and have begun to reign.
> 18 The nations were angry,
>   and your wrath has come.
> *The time has come for judging the dead,*
>   *and for rewarding your servants the prophets*
> and your people who revere your name,
>   both great and small—
> and for destroying those who destroy the earth."

Revelation 11:15–18 notes that when this seventh and final trumpet sounds:

- The kingdom of the world will become "the kingdom of our Lord and his Messiah" (v. 15).
- The eternal reign of Jesus will begin (v. 15).
- The time will come for "judging the dead," for "rewarding your servants the prophets," and for rewarding "your people who revere your name" (v. 18).

As I noted previously, I've concluded that the events described in Rev 11:15–18 are referring to Jesus' return and the judgment that follows—the same time of judgment Jesus was warning about in the parables in Matt 24 and 25—culminating in this (Matt 25:31–33, 46):

> 31 "When the Son of Man comes in his glory, and all the angels with him, he will sit on his glorious throne. 32 All the nations will be gathered before him, and *he will separate the people one from another as a shepherd separates the sheep from the goats.* 33 He will put the sheep on his right and the goats on his left . . . 46 "Then they [the goats] will go away to eternal punishment, but the righteous [the sheep] to eternal life."

As I also noted, the period of judgment described in both Matt 25:31–46 and Rev 11:15–18 seems to be the same time of judgment Jesus was describing in the Parable of the Weeds in Matt 13:24–30—a time of judgment that occurs when the harvest at the end of the age takes place.

The passages above are connected by their use of similar images to describe what takes place, by similarities in the event described, and by consistency in what followers of Jesus are encouraged to do as they wait for this event to occur. That is sufficient for me to conclude these passages are describing the same event.

If this is so—if the last trumpet Paul was referring to in 1 Cor 15:52 is the same as the seventh and final trumpet in Rev 11:15—it provides additional support for my conclusion that Rev 11:15–18 is the first of three accounts of the return of Jesus in Revelation.

JESUS' "SECRET" RETURN

I mentioned earlier why I've concluded that Jesus returns only once, and that when he does, "All the peoples of the earth will . . . see the Son of Man coming on the clouds of heaven" (Matt 24:30). There are other passages in Scripture that support my observation that Jesus' return will not be unseen. Matthew 16:24–27 is one of them:

> 24 Then Jesus said to his disciples, "Whoever wants to be my disciple must deny themselves and take up their cross and follow me. 25 For whoever wants to save their life will lose it, but whoever loses their life for me will find it. 26 What good will it be for someone to gain the whole world, yet forfeit their soul? Or what can anyone give in exchange for their soul? *27 For the Son of Man is going to come in his Father's glory with his angels, and then he will reward each person according to what they have done."*

The focus of Matt 16:24–27 seems to be what Jesus told his disciples they must do to enter into a saving relationship with him and remain in that relationship. They must, for example, deny themselves and do whatever "cross-bearing" Jesus required (v. 24). They must also be willing to give up their own lives for the sake of Jesus (v. 25). Jesus then told his disciples that he would return someday and that, when he did, he would reward each person according to what they have done (v. 27).

The following are ways Matt 16:24–27 connects to passages already discussed:

- Angels will accompany Jesus when he returns (v. 27; Matt 24:30–31; 2 Thess 1:7).

- Jesus' return will be followed by each person being judged based on what they did while Jesus was away (v. 27; Matt 25:31–46; Rev 11:15–18).

- Those who follow Jesus are urged to do what is commendable in Jesus' eyes as they wait for Jesus to return (vv. 24–26; Matt 7:21, 24:13; 2 Pet 3:11).

Acts 1:1–11 also describes Jesus' return in a way I find significant:

> 1 In my former book, Theophilus, I wrote about all that Jesus began to do and to teach 2 until the day he was taken up to heaven, after giving instructions through the Holy Spirit to the apostles he had chosen. 3 After his suffering, he presented himself to them and gave many convincing proofs that he was alive. He appeared to them over a period of forty days and spoke about the kingdom of God. 4 On one occasion, while he was eating with them, he gave them this command: "Do not leave Jerusalem, but wait for the gift my Father promised, which you have heard me speak about. 5 For John baptized with water, but in a few days you will be baptized with the Holy Spirit."
>
> 6 Then they gathered around him and asked him, "*Lord, are you at this time going to restore the kingdom to Israel?*"
>
> 7 He said to them: "*It is not for you to know the times or dates the Father has set* by his own authority. 8 But you will receive power when the Holy Spirit comes on you; and *you will be my witnesses in Jerusalem, and in all Judea and Samaria, and to the ends of the earth.*"
>
> 9 After he said this, *he was taken up before their very eyes, and a cloud hid him from their sight.*
>
> 10 They were looking intently up into the sky as he was going, when suddenly two men dressed in white stood beside them. 11 "Men of Galilee," they said, "why do you stand here looking into the sky? *This same Jesus, who has been taken from you into heaven, will come back in the same way you have seen him go into heaven.*"

There are two things I find interesting about the above passage when considering its relevance to the return of Jesus. First, Jesus' disciples wanted to know when Jesus was going to establish his kingdom (v. 6), just like they did when Jesus was speaking to them during the week before his arrest and crucifixion (Matt 24:3). They thought here, as they had then, that Jesus was going to establish his kingdom soon—perhaps in a matter of days.

Jesus reminded his disciples that knowing the date or time when he was going to establish his kingdom was not to be their concern (v. 7). Their sole focus as they waited for Jesus to return was to be on the mission he'd given to them. That mission was to be Jesus' witnesses in Jerusalem, in the regions surrounding it, and to the entire world (v. 8).

I also find it interesting to note how Jesus left them that day and how this compares to the way Jesus is going to return. Jesus' disciples saw Jesus visibly rise up to the sky until hidden from their sight by a cloud (v. 9). As they gazed up into the sky, two angels appeared and told them that Jesus would return in the same way they'd just seen him leave (v. 11).

If Jesus' return is going to be a mirror image of the way he left his disciples that day, we would expect Jesus to appear visibly in or on some clouds, just as described in these verses:

- "Then will appear the sign of the Son of Man in heaven. And then *all the peoples* of the earth *will* mourn when they *see the Son of Man coming on the clouds of heaven*, with power and great glory" (Matt 24:30).

- "'Look, he is coming with the clouds,'
  and 'every eye will see him,
  even those who pierced him';
  and all peoples on earth 'will mourn because of him.'
  So shall it be! Amen" (Rev 1:7).

- 14 "I looked, and there before me was a white cloud, and seated on the cloud was one like a son of man with a crown of gold on his head and a sharp sickle in his hand. 15 Then another angel came out of the temple and called in a loud voice to him who was *sitting on the cloud*, 'Take your sickle and reap, because the time to reap has come, for the harvest of the earth is ripe.' 16 So he who was *seated on the cloud* swung his sickle over the earth, and the earth was harvested" (Rev 14:14–16).

The Bible consistently articulates that, when Jesus returns, it will not be an event hidden from anyone.

A BLOODIED WARRIOR

One question I consider relevant when considering Jesus' second coming is if there could be some conditions in the world that would prompt or compel Jesus to return. Rather than listing some possible answers to this, I want to draw attention to two passages that seem to speak to this and explain my understanding of them.

Isaiah 63:1–6 is the first of the two.

> 1 Who is this coming from Edom,
>   from Bozrah, with his *garments stained crimson*?

The Final Trumpet, Jesus' "Secret" Return, and a Bloodied Warrior

> Who is this, robed in splendor,
>   striding forward in the greatness of his strength?
> "It is I, proclaiming victory,
>   mighty to save."
> 2 Why are your *garments red,*
>   *like those of one treading the winepress*?
> 3 "*I have trodden the winepress alone*;
>   from the nations no one was with me.
> I trampled them in my anger
>   and trod them down in my wrath;
> their *blood spattered my garments,*
>   and I stained all my clothing.
> 4 It was for me the day of vengeance;
>   the year for me to redeem had come.
> 5 *I looked, but there was no one to help,*
>   I was appalled that no one gave support;
> so my own arm achieved salvation for me,
>   and my own wrath sustained me.
> 6 *I trampled the nations in my anger;*
>   *in my wrath I made them drunk*
>   *and poured their blood on the ground.*"

Isaiah 63:1–6 describes a time when a warrior from Edom (v. 1) tramples the nations of the world in anger (v. 6).

The first thing I want to point out about this passage is the images it uses to describe this warrior and where these images show up elsewhere in Scripture. Note, for example, how this warrior's garments are described:

- They are "stained crimson" (v. 1).
- They are "red, like those of one treading a winepress" (v. 2).
- They have been splattered with blood (v. 3).

The above images show up in Rev 19:11–13 as well:

> 11 I saw heaven standing open and there before me was a white horse, whose rider is called Faithful and True. With justice he judges and wages war. 12 His eyes are like blazing fire, and on his head are many crowns. He has a name written on him that no one knows but he himself. 13 *He is dressed in a robe dipped in blood*, and his name is the Word of God.

Note that the warrior described in Rev 19:11–13 is wearing a "robe dipped in blood" (v. 13). This is similar to the image in Isa 63:1 of a warrior whose "garments [are] stained crimson."

Because of these similarities, I've concluded that Isa 63:1–6 and Rev 19:11–13 are describing the same warrior.

Here are other characteristics of the warrior in Isa 63:1–6 that I consider significant:

- He trods (beats with his feet) grapes in a winepress, symbolizing what he is doing to the nations and why his garments are spattered with blood (v. 3).

- He tramples the nations in anger and in wrath and pours out their blood upon the ground (v. 6).

The above images are also found in Rev 14:14–20:

> 14 I looked, and there before me was a white cloud, and seated on the cloud was one like a son of man with a crown of gold on his head and a sharp sickle in his hand. 15 Then another angel came out of the temple and called in a loud voice to him who was sitting on the cloud, "Take your sickle and reap, because the time to reap has come, for the harvest of the earth is ripe." 16 So he who was seated on the cloud swung his sickle over the earth, and the earth was harvested.
>
> 17 Another angel came out of the temple in heaven, and he too had a sharp sickle. 18 Still another angel, who had charge of the fire, came from the altar and called in a loud voice to him who had the sharp sickle, "Take your sharp sickle and gather the clusters of grapes from the earth's vine, because its grapes are ripe." 19 *The angel swung his sickle on the earth, gathered its grapes and threw them into the great winepress of God's wrath. 20 They were trampled in the winepress outside the city, and blood flowed out of the press, rising as high as the horses' bridles for a distance of 1,600 stadia.*

I noted previously why I've concluded the one "seated on the cloud" in Rev 14:14 is Jesus, why Rev 14:14–20 seems to be describing the same event recorded in Matt 24:30–31 (the return of Jesus), and why this passage in Revelation could be the second of three descriptions of Jesus' return in Revelation. I also noted that this passage in Revelation compares Jesus' return to a harvest—the same harvest Jesus was alluding to in the Parable of the Weeds.

What I want to draw attention to here is that the harvest in Rev 14:14–20 is described as a gathering of grapes that are thrown into "the great winepress of God's wrath" (v. 19). These grapes are then "trampled in the winepress outside the city," resulting in blood flowing out of the press that rises as high as horses' bridles (v. 20).

Could this be the same winepress of wrath described in Isa 63:3? And could this be why this warrior's clothes are covered with blood?

Note as well what Rev 19:14–16 records:

> 14 The armies of heaven were following him, riding on white horses and dressed in fine linen, white and clean. 15 Coming out of his mouth is a sharp sword with which to strike down the nations. "He will rule them with an iron scepter." *He treads the winepress of the fury of the wrath of God Almighty.* 16 On his robe and on his thigh he has this name written:
>
> KING OF KINGS AND LORD OF LORDS.

The verses above describe Jesus—the King of kings and Lord of lords—treading "the winepress of the fury of the wrath of God Almighty" (v. 15), a winepress that is mentioned in both Rev 14:19 and Isa 63:3.

Based on these comparisons, it seems that all three passages—Isa 63:1–6, Rev 14:14–20, and Rev 19:11–21—are describing the same event.

But why does the warrior described in Isa 63:1–6 act this way? Why does he tread the nations in anger? A clue to that can be found in these two verses:

- "I have trodden the winepress alone;
  from the nations *no one was with me*" (Isa 63:3).

- "I looked, but *there was no one to help*,
  I was appalled that *no one gave support*;
  so my own arm achieved salvation for me,
  and my own wrath sustained me" (Isa 63:5).

What this warrior ends up doing he apparently does alone. Although he looked for help, no one was willing to assist him. He was "appalled that no one gave support" (v. 5).

Why was this warrior asking for help? Was there something going on that others could have fixed if they were willing to intervene? What was lacking in those who refused to support him?

To answer those questions, I want to draw attention to Isa 59:1–20, a passage that appears to be connected to Isa 63:1–6. I realize this is a lengthy passage. But I consider the details important if one wants to understand at least one reason Jesus may feel compelled to return:

> 1 Surely the arm of the LORD is not too short to save,
> nor his ear too dull to hear.
> 2 But your *iniquities* have separated
> you from your God;
> your *sins* have hidden his face from you,
> so that he will not hear.
> 3 For your *hands are stained with blood,*
> your fingers with guilt.
> Your *lips have spoken falsely,*
> and your tongue mutters wicked things.
> 4 *No one calls for justice;*
> no one pleads a case with integrity.
> They rely on empty arguments, *they utter lies;*
> they conceive trouble and *give birth to evil.*
> 5 *They hatch the eggs of vipers*
> and spin a spider's web.
> Whoever eats their eggs will die,
> and when one is broken, an adder is hatched.
> 6 Their cobwebs are useless for clothing;
> they cannot cover themselves with what they make.
> *Their deeds are evil* deeds,
> and *acts of violence are in their hands.*
> 7 *Their feet rush into sin;*
> they are *swift to shed innocent blood.*
> They *pursue evil schemes;*
> acts of *violence mark their ways.*
> 8 *The way of peace they do not know;*
> there is *no justice* in their paths.
> They have turned them into crooked roads;
> no one who walks along them will know peace.
> 9 So *justice is far from us,*
> and *righteousness does not reach us.*
> *We look for light, but all is darkness;*
> for brightness, but we walk in deep shadows.
> 10 *Like the blind* we grope along the wall,
> feeling our way like people without eyes.
> At midday *we stumble* as if it were twilight;
> among the strong, *we are like the dead.*
> 11 We all growl like bears;
> we moan mournfully like doves.

> We look for justice, but find none;
> for deliverance, but it is far away.
> 12 For our offenses are many in your sight,
> and our sins testify against us.
> Our offenses are ever with us,
> and we acknowledge our iniquities:
> 13 *rebellion and treachery against the* LORD,
> turning our backs on our God,
> *inciting revolt and oppression,*
> uttering lies our hearts have conceived.
> 14 So *justice is driven back,*
> and righteousness stands at a distance;
> truth has stumbled in the streets,
> honesty cannot enter.
> 15 *Truth is nowhere to be found,*
> *and whoever shuns evil becomes a prey.*
> The LORD looked and was displeased
> that there was *no justice.*
> 16 *He saw that there was no one,*
> *he was appalled that there was no one to intervene;*
> so his own arm achieved salvation for him,
> and his own righteousness sustained him.
> 17 He put on righteousness as his breastplate,
> and the helmet of salvation on his head;
> *he put on the garments of vengeance*
> and wrapped himself in zeal as in a cloak.
> 18 According to what they have done,
> *so will he repay*
> *wrath to his enemies*
> *and retribution to his foes;*
> he will repay the islands their due.
> 19 From the west, people will fear the name of the LORD,
> and from the rising of the sun, they will revere his glory.
> For he will come like a pent-up flood
> that the breath of the LORD drives along.
> 20 "*The Redeemer will come to Zion,*
> *to those in Jacob who repent of their sins,*"
> declares the LORD.

One thing described in Isa 59:1–20 is the Lord putting on "garments of vengeance" (v. 17) so that he can "repay wrath to his enemies and retribution to his foes" (v. 18). This is similar to the warrior in Isa 63 who calls the day he tramples the nations in anger a "day of vengeance" (Isa 63:3–4).

Also, note that, just like the warrior in Isa 63:5 who was "appalled that no one gave support," in Isa 59:16, the Lord "was appalled that there was no one to intervene".

Based on these similarities, it appears that Isa 59:1–20 and Isa 63:1–6 are describing the same warrior and the same event. If this is so, then they could be describing the same trampling of grapes that takes place in Rev 14:14–20, the same coming of the warrior—the King of kings—described in Rev 19:11–21, and the same harvest Jesus was referring to in the Parable of the Weeds.

This still doesn't answer the question of why Jesus may feel compelled to return. But it may have to do with the moral state of the world at that time. According to Isa 59:1–20, this world will be characterized by

- iniquity and sin that separates people from God (v. 2);
- hands stained with blood; lips that speak falsely (v. 3);
- no calls for justice; giving birth to evil (v. 4);
- evil and violence (v. 6);
- feet that rush to sin; people being swift to shed innocent blood; the pursuit of evil schemes (v. 7);
- ways of peace unknown (v. 8);
- justice and righteousness that are far off; people who walk in darkness rather than light (v. 9);
- people stumbling like the blind and living as if they are dead (v. 10);
- rebellion against God; inciting revolt and oppression (v. 13); and
- a lack of truth and justice (v. 15).

Some may look at the above list of evils and conclude this is what characterizes our world today. They may also conclude that if this is so, then Jesus' return cannot be far off. But I want to insert here my personal thoughts about the state of the world we live in and how this ties to Isa 59:1–20.

Although there are regions of the world today that seem to be characterized by the evils described in Isa 59:1–20, I don't believe these evils characterize our world as a whole. And though there have been times in the past when the moral condition of the world may have seemed to be better than it is today, there have also been times and places when it was worse. So what conditions might prompt Jesus to intervene in such an extreme way that blood literally or symbolically drips from his robe?

It could be at a time when things are so bad that, if left to our own resources, we will self-destruct.

I don't think we are there yet. We may not even be close. But based on the verse in Isa 59:16 that says, "He was appalled that there was no one to intervene," and the one in Isa 63:5 that says, "I looked, but there was no one to help; I was appalled that no one gave support," it seems to me that Jesus is looking for help to keep the world from getting to the moral condition described in Isa 59:1–20.

What can we do to give Jesus the help he is looking for? Perhaps it is by not being found guilty of engaging in any of the evils described in Isa 59:1–20. Perhaps it is by being committed to live in obedience to God's will and his standards of righteousness. Perhaps it is by heeding Jesus' call to influence the world in positive, God-affirming ways. Perhaps it is by being salt and light in our world so that those who see our good deeds will glorify our Father in heaven (Matt 5:13–16).

Although Scripture clearly articulates that Jesus' return is certain and inevitable, these verses in Isaiah seem to suggest that we can affect the timing of it. We can do this, perhaps, by continuing to do what is commendable in God's eyes, so that Jesus will not find it necessary to return to fix what is broken, to make right what is wrong, or to judge those who have rejected him and his standards of righteousness.

Chapter 7

The Three Accounts of the Return of Jesus in Revelation

Blessed is the one who reads aloud the words of this prophecy, and blessed are those who hear it and take to heart what is written in it, because the time is near.

REVELATION 1:3

ONE COMMON INTERPRETATION OF Revelation is that it describes, for the most part, what will happen in the world following the rapture of the church.

As I noted in previous chapters, many Christians believe the rapture of the church will result in the removal of all followers of Jesus from the face of the Earth, and that this will be followed by seven years of tribulation and judgment for those remaining. Those who hold to this view often conclude that Revelation, beginning in chapter 4 and continuing nearly to the end, provides a chronological description of what will happen to those left behind in the seven years that follow the rapture.

I've concluded that Revelation is not describing what will happen *after* Christians have been taken from this world by Jesus. It seems to me that Revelation is primarily describing what Christians will witness or experience *prior* to the return of Jesus. Some of the events Revelation describes are common to all—events everyone sharing the same field will experience before the harvest at the end of the age. Some of the events described in Revelation will happen only to those who are enemies of God. But some of

The Three Accounts of the Return of Jesus in Revelation

the events described will be experienced only by those who are followers of Jesus.

In order to understand why I've come to this determination, and additionally, why I've concluded there are three accounts of the return of Jesus in Revelation, it's important to note how prophecies in the Bible are recorded in general.

Although some prophecies provide a chronological description of future events, most provide only a piece of a puzzle that won't be completely understood until that puzzle is finished. The error many seem to make regarding Revelation, at least from chapter 4 onwards, is to conclude that it is a chronological timeline of end-time events. This is not required by the text, however, nor does it fit the pattern of how prophecies in the Bible are commonly recorded.

The book of Daniel is a good example of a more typical way prophecies are recorded. Daniel explained the meaning of a statue that Nebuchadnezzar, the king of Babylon, saw in one of his dreams (Dan 2). This statue had a head of gold, arms and chest of silver, belly and thighs of bronze, and legs of iron. A rock then smashed the statue's legs, causing the rest to crumble (vv. 31–35).

Daniel told the king that the head of the statue symbolized Babylon, and the rest symbolized three kingdoms that were yet to come. These three are typically understood to be Medo-Persia, Greece, and Rome.

The book of Daniel continues by noting other dreams and visions Daniel had or interpreted, as well as prophecies communicated to him by other messengers of God. Most of these prophecies provided more details about the four kingdoms symbolized by the statue.

Here is a summary of these prophecies and visions:

- Daniel interpreted a dream Nebuchadnezzar had that prophesied the loss of the king's sanity due to his failure to acknowledge that God was the source of his wealth and power (Dan 4).

- Daniel interpreted the meaning of "writing on the wall" from a divine hand that prophesied Babylon would be given to the Medes and Persians due to the arrogance of King Belshazzar, Nebuchadnezzar's son (Dan 5).

- Daniel received a vision in a dream of four beasts: a lion, a bear, a leopard, and an unidentified but terrifying beast. Each of these represented one of the kingdoms symbolized by the statue in Nebuchadnezzar's dream (Dan 7).

- Daniel received a vision of a ram and goat. This dream focused on two of the four kingdoms symbolized by the statue. The ram symbolized Medo-Persia. The goat symbolized Greece (Dan 8).
- Daniel received an explanation by a divine being of when, in the midst of the rise and fall of the four kingdoms symbolized by the statue, the Jews would be forgiven for their sins (Dan 9).
- Daniel received more details by a divine being regarding the Persian, Greek, and Roman periods (Dan 10–11), as well as a time typically understood to be the end of the age (Dan 12).

What I want to emphasize here regarding the prophecies in Daniel is that, though an individual chapter may provide a chronological description of future events, when considering the book as a whole, these prophecies are not presented in a continuous timeline. The prophecies in Daniel begin with a basic framework—the interpretation of a dream regarding a statue—and proceed in subsequent chapters to provide more details about what the statue symbolizes. For the most part, the prophecies in Daniel are additive in nature, not sequential, adding to or clarifying something revealed earlier.

This is similar to my conclusion regarding the role the Parable of the Weeds plays in understanding other end-time passages. This parable provides a framework that Jesus and others fleshed out in subsequent discourses or writings, culminating in a more robust description of end-time events in Revelation. But if the prophecies in Revelation fit the pattern of how the prophecies in Daniel were recorded, we would expect them to be additive as well.

There is another thing that needs to be kept in mind when discussing the intent and structure of Revelation. It is its context.

Daniel was writing to Jews living in exile in Babylon. One of his reasons for doing so was to pass along prophecies he received regarding what the future held for the Jews and their descendants so that they would know what to expect prior to coming of the "Anointed One" (Dan 9:25)—prior to Jesus coming in the flesh to dwell among them (John 1:14).

It seems to me that John wrote Revelation for the benefit of Christians in all generations, beginning with those living in the first century, in order to describe what followers of Jesus can expect to experience prior to Jesus' return.

As I elaborate on this, I will divide Revelation into these six sections and themes:

The Three Accounts of the Return of Jesus in Revelation

- Section 1: Who John Was Writing to and Why He Was Writing to Them (Rev 1).
- Section 2: What Was Happening Then: The Good and the Bad (Rev 2–3).
- Section 3: What Christians Will Experience Prior to the Return of Jesus (Rev 4–11).
- Section 4: What Satan Wants to Accomplish (Rev 12–14).
- Section 5: What Will Eventually Happen to Jesus' Enemies (Rev 15–19).
- Section 6: What Will Happen After All of This (Rev 20–22).

SECTION 1: WHO JOHN WAS WRITING TO AND WHY HE WAS WRITING TO THEM (REV 1)

In order to understand what John was trying to convey through the prophecies recorded in Revelation and what this has to do with us, the first thing we need to note is who John was writing to and what he wanted them to know.

The answer regarding who John was writing to is clear. John was writing "to the seven churches in the province of Asia" (Rev 1:4).

John was writing to seven first-century churches that were located in modern-day Turkey. But though his primary audience was Gentile and Jewish Christians associated with these churches, that doesn't mean that what he revealed isn't relevant for Christians in other times or places. What it does mean is that Revelation is best understood in the context of the audience to which it was originally addressed.

What these Christians wanted to know, and perhaps needed to know, can be discerned by looking at a number of verses. For example, they likely understood that Jesus would return some day but may have needed a reminder of this (Rev 1:7):

> "Look, he is coming with the clouds," and "every eye will see him, even those who pierced him"; and all peoples on earth "will mourn because of him." So shall it be! Amen.

As they waited for Jesus to return, it seems they were suffering (Rev 1:9):

> I, John, your brother and *companion in the suffering* and kingdom and patient endurance that are ours in Jesus.

These verses provide some clues about what the focus of John's letter to these Christians was going to be as he considered their circumstances and concerns:

- 1 "The revelation from Jesus Christ, which God gave him to show his servants *what must soon take place*. He made it known by sending his angel to his servant John, 2 who testifies to everything he saw—that is, the word of God and the testimony of Jesus Christ. 3 Blessed is the one who reads aloud the words of this prophecy, and blessed are those who hear it and take to heart what is written in it, *because the time is near*" (Rev 1:1–3).

- "Write, therefore, what you have seen, *what is now and what will take place later*" (Rev 1:19).

Many Christians in those days likely wanted to know what lay ahead of them. In that regard, they were little different than Christians today who want to know the same thing. John wrote that he was revealing to them "what must *soon* take place" (Rev 1:1), as well as "what is *now* and what will take place *later*" (Rev 1:19).

It's apparent when noting this that some of the events John described were occurring at that time. They were happening *now* from the perspective of those he was writing to. And though some of the events John described wouldn't occur until *later*, many were going to happen *soon*.

And by *soon*, I don't think John meant in thousands or hundreds of years. Many of the events described in Revelation were going to take place *soon* from the perspective of those John was originally writing to.

This understanding of the contextual meaning of *soon* helps in appreciating the urgency in which John pleas for those reading his letter to "take to heart what is written in it, because the time is near" (Rev 1:3). The gravity of John's plea doesn't make sense if the events he was writing about weren't going to occur until a far distant time. It also doesn't make sense if, by *near*, that John was referring to the return of Jesus, since Jesus' return, from his perspective, was far off and not near.

John was urging those he was writing to at that time to read and heed what he was saying, as many of the events he was describing were near.

SECTION 2: WHAT WAS HAPPENING THEN: THE GOOD AND THE BAD (REV 2-3)

The next two chapters of Revelation describe characteristics of the seven churches John was writing to. Five of these churches had significant issues. Two were doing fairly well.

Here was what Jesus had against the five:

- The church in Ephesus had forsaken the love it had at first (Rev 2:4).
- Some Christians at the church in Pergamum were embracing false teaching (Rev 2:14–15).
- The church in Thyatira had allowed a false prophet to infiltrate it (Rev 2:20).
- The church in Sardis was spiritually dead (Rev 3:1).
- The church in Laodicea was "wretched, pitiful, poor, blind, and naked" (Rev 3:17).

This is what was going to happen to each of these five churches if what characterized them didn't change:

- The church in Ephesus would lose its lampstand, symbolizing perhaps that it would no longer be a light to the world (Rev 2:5).
- Some Christians in Pergamum would find Jesus fighting against them (Rev 2:16).
- Some Christians in Thyatira would suffer; some would die (Rev 2:22–23).
- Jesus would come like a thief to those in Sardis who did not wake up and repent (Rev 3:3).
- The church in Laodicea would be spit out of God's mouth (Rev 3:16).

This is what characterized the other two churches:

- The church in Smyrna was spiritually rich but was going to suffer persecution (Rev 2:9–10).
- The church in Philadelphia was weak but had kept God's word and not denied his name (Rev 3:8).

This is how these churches would be rewarded if they remained this way:

- The church in Smyrna would be given life as its victor's crown (Rev 2:10).
- The church in Philadelphia would be spared from the hour of trial that was to come (Rev 3:10).

Those associated with these seven churches likely understood that Jesus was speaking to them personally. And what Jesus was telling them is what could or would happen to them as a result of their good character or lack thereof. That doesn't mean what John wrote isn't relevant for Christians in other times or places. The lessons these two chapters of Revelation convey are timeless. Christians today are called to be like those in these churches that were doing well and to avoid being like those who were not doing well.

SECTION 3: WHAT CHRISTIANS WILL EXPERIENCE PRIOR TO THE RETURN OF JESUS (REV 4-11)

When I noted in chapter 2 questions Jesus' disciples had about his return and the end of the age, as well as questions Christians today may have about Jesus' return, I mentioned three I considered relevant. As a reminder, they are:

- What are some challenges we will face before the end comes?
- Why will we experience these?
- How does God want us to respond when they take place?

Jesus answered these questions to an extent. The letters written by Paul, Peter, and John do as well.

It seems to me that Revelation, beginning with Rev 4, provides answers to these three questions that are more in depth.

The focus of chapters 4 through 11 of Revelation seems to be in response to the first question, "What are some challenges we will face before the end comes?" What is described in these eight chapters are events that may have been occurring at that time, that would occur soon from the perspective of the original readers, or that would not occur until much later. From our perspective, some of these events may already have taken place, some may be occurring today, and some are still in the future.

The Three Accounts of the Return of Jesus in Revelation

The following lists five of these events. They were revealed to John when the first five of seven seals of a scroll he saw in a vision (Rev 5:1–5) were opened by Jesus (Rev 6:1–11):

- Seal #1: A warrior on a white horse rides "out as a conqueror bent on conquest" (Rev 6:1–2).
- Seal #2: A rider on a red horse is "given power to take peace from the earth and to make people kill each other" (Rev 6:3–4).
- Seal #3: A rider on a black horse causes famine, resulting in "two pounds of wheat for a day's wages, and six pounds of barley for a day's wages" (Rev 6:5–6).
- Seal #4: A rider on a pale horse named Death, along with a rider on another horse named Hades, are "given power over a fourth of the earth to kill by sword, famine and plague, and by the wild beasts of the earth" (Rev 6:7–8).
- Seal #5: Those "slain because of the word of God" wonder how long it will be before God judges the inhabitants of the earth and avenges their blood. They are told that they need to wait a little longer, "until the full number of their fellow servants, their brothers and sisters, were killed just as they had been" (Rev 6:9–11).

The events John described as these five seals were opened are similar to the difficulties Jesus told his disciples that they and other followers of him were going to experience prior to his return. For example:

- There will be wars and rumors of wars. "Such things must happen, but the end is still to come" (Matt 24:6; seal #1).
- "Nation will rise against nation, and kingdom against kingdom" (Matt 24:7; seal #2).
- "There will be famines" (Matt 24:7; seal #3).
- "Nation will rise against nation, and kingdom against kingdom. There will be great earthquakes, famines and pestilences in various places, and fearful events and great signs from heaven" (Luke 21:10–11; seal #4).
- "You will be handed over to be persecuted and put to death, and you will be hated by all nations because of me" (Matt 24:9; seal #5).

The events described by Jesus in the verses above, as well as the ones described by John when the first five seals were broken, are not uncommon. They have occurred in the past, are occurring today, and will continue to occur until Jesus returns. What is uncommon is what John described when the sixth seal was opened (Rev 6:12–14):

> 12 I watched as he opened the sixth seal. There was a great earthquake. The *sun turned black* like sackcloth made of goat hair, the whole *moon turned blood red*, 13 and the *stars in the sky fell to earth*, as figs drop from a fig tree when shaken by a strong wind. 14 The *heavens receded like a scroll being rolled up*, and every mountain and island was removed from its place.

Although there are times when the sun turns black (e.g., during a full solar eclipse), and times when the moon looks blood red (e.g., during some lunar eclipses), what is described in Rev 6:12–14 when the sixth seal is opened is something that has not occurred to the extent John described.

Matthew 24:29 includes similar images:

> Immediately after the distress of those days
> "the *sun will be darkened*,
>   and the *moon will not give its light*;
> the *stars will fall from the sky*,
>   and the *heavenly bodies will be shaken*."

Because of the similarities in the images Matt 24:29 and Rev 6:12–14 use to describe what happens to the sun, moon, stars, and other heavenly bodies, I'm inclined to conclude that they are referring to the same event.

What John described when these first six seals were opened is not the end of troubles for Christians or others living in the world, however. When the seventh seal was opened (Rev 8:1), these additional events were revealed to John:

- Hail and fire mixed with blood come down from heaven; a third of the world is burned up (Rev 8:7).
- A third of the seas turns to blood, a third of all sea creatures die, and a third of all ships are destroyed (Rev 8:8–9).
- A third of all rivers and springs turn bitter. Many die because of this (Rev 8:10–11).
- A third of the night and day are without light (Rev 8:12).
- Those not sealed by God are tortured by locusts (Rev 9:3–4).

- A third of those unrepentant are killed by plagues of fire, smoke, and sulfur (Rev 9:18–21).

Other challenging events were described by John in Rev 10 and 11.

This section of Revelation concludes with what I consider to be the first account of the return of Jesus in Revelation (Rev 11:15–18). This will be the moment when "the kingdom of the world has become the kingdom of our Lord and of his Messiah, and he will reign for ever and ever" (v. 15). It will also be when "the time has come for judging the dead, and for rewarding your servants the prophets and your people who revere your name, both great and small—and for destroying those who destroy the earth" (v. 18).

As I noted in previous chapters, it appears that the period of judgment described in Rev 11:18 is the same time of judgment described Matt 25:31–46—the moment when Jesus returns, sits on a throne, and separates the righteous from the unrighteous, sending each to their respective eternal destination. I've also concluded that the separation of the righteous from the unrighteous that takes place at that time is the same separation symbolized by the Parable of the Weeds—a separation that takes place when the harvest at the end of the age occurs.

It seems to me that the purpose of Rev 4–11 is to remind us that we are destined to experience difficult and challenging times prior to the return of Jesus. We should not be surprised or distressed when these take place, however. Instead, we should consider them inevitable.

SECTION 4: WHAT SATAN WANTS TO ACCOMPLISH (REV 12-14)

Christians will experience difficulties when the events described in chapters 4 through 11 of Revelation take place. What will make these even more challenging is what Satan wants to accomplish in the midst of them.

There are spiritual forces in this world arrayed against Christians, as well as against those who are not. These forces are intent on keeping people separated from God or, for those already in a saving relationship with Jesus, destroying that relationship.

Ephesians 6:12 notes something Paul had to say about these forces:

> For our struggle is not against flesh and blood, but against the rulers, against the authorities, against the powers of this dark world and against the spiritual forces of evil in the heavenly realms.

The battle described in the above verse began in the garden of Eden. It is first alluded to in a prophecy recorded in Gen 3:14–19. This prophecy describes what was going to happen following Satan's success in getting Adam and Eve to eat fruit from a tree God had forbidden them to eat from (Gen 2:17; 3:1–13).

Here is part of that prophecy (Gen 3:14–15):

> 14 So the LORD God said to the serpent, "Because you have done this,
> "Cursed are you above all livestock
>   and all wild animals!
> You will crawl on your belly
>   and you will eat dust
>   all the days of your life.
> 15 *And I will put enmity*
>   *between you and the woman,*
>   *and between your offspring and hers;*
> *he will crush your head,*
>   *and you will strike his heel."*

Adam's and Eve's disobedience would result in hostility between Satan and Eve's offspring. Eve's most significant descendant in this regard would be Jesus. The enmity between Satan and Jesus would result in attempts by Satan to undermine God's plan to redeem the world. Satan might even think at times that he was victorious in this, when all he'd actually done was to nip Jesus on the heel. Satan's head would eventually be crushed by Jesus when Jesus rose from the dead days after he was crucified.

Revelation 12–14 seem to be elaborating on some aspects of the conflict between Satan and the offspring of Eve, as well as Satan's continued attempts to thwart God's plan of redemption.

Here are images Rev 12 uses to describe this conflict and what they seem to symbolize:

- A woman with "a crown of twelve stars on her head" (v. 1), who seems to represent the nation of Israel and its twelve tribes,[1] is pregnant with a child (v. 2), "a son, a male child, who 'will rule all the nations with an iron scepter'" (v. 5), an image that symbolizes Jesus.

---

1. This is similar to Joseph's dream in which the sun, moon, and eleven stars bowed down to him. This symbolized Joseph's father, mother, and eleven brothers (Gen 37:9–10), and foreshadowed the day they would bow down to Joseph after he rose to power in Egypt.

- A "dragon with seven heads and ten horns" (v. 3), symbolizing Satan (v. 9), stands in front of the woman in the hope that he "might devour her child the moment he was born" (v. 4). His attempt to do so is unsuccessful.[2]

- The woman successfully flees "into the wilderness to a place prepared for her by God, where she might be taken care of for 1,260 days" (v. 6). This may be referring to the time Herod attempted to kill Jesus by ordering the murder of all male children in Bethlehem two years old or younger. Herod's attempt to kill Jesus failed when Joseph and Mary fled to Egypt, taking Jesus with them (Matt 2:1–18).

- It describes once again the dragon's attempt to destroy the woman and her child, and the woman fleeing to a place "in the wilderness where she would be taken care of for a time, times and half a time [1,260 days], out of the serpents' reach" (vv. 13–14).

- Having failed to stop the birth of Jesus or kill him afterwards, "the dragon was enraged at the woman and went off to wage war against the rest of her offspring—those who keep God's commands and hold fast their testimony about Jesus" (v. 17).

Revelation 12:17 states unequivocally that Satan has declared war on Christians.

What follows in Rev 13 are prophecies regarding what Satan will be doing in order to win some battles in this war. This chapter of Revelation begins with a description of a beast that is given a mouth "to blaspheme God, and to slander his name and his dwelling place and those who live in heaven" (v. 6). This beast is "given power to wage war against God's holy people and to conquer them" (v. 7). Eventually, "All inhabitants of the earth will worship the beast—all whose names have not been written in the Lamb's book of life, the Lamb who was slain from the creation of the world" (v. 8).

Revelation 13:9–10 describes the threat this beast poses for Christians and how they are urged to respond when they face this threat:

---

2. Satan may have been trying to prevent the birth of Jesus centuries earlier through Pharaoh's edict for every newborn Hebrew boy to be thrown into the Nile (Exod 1:22), as well as through Haman's request to King Xerxes to be allowed kill all the Jews living in Persia (Esth 3:8–11).

9 Whoever has ears, let them hear.
10 "If anyone is to go into captivity,
into captivity they will go.
If anyone is to be killed with the sword,
with the sword they will be killed."
This calls for patient endurance and faithfulness on the part of God's people.

What were Christians going to experience when this beast showed up? As John noted, some would be taken captive and some killed.

How were Christians to respond when they experienced this and the other challenges this beast posed?

With "patient endurance and faithfulness."

Although it's possible the beast in Rev 13 symbolizes a single end-time individual, nation, or group of nations, the context does not require this limitation. This beast could just as easily be any individual, group, or nation Satan uses to attack Christians. This would certainly fit the circumstances of some of those John was writing to who John called companions "in the suffering and kingdom and patient endurance that are ours in Jesus" (Rev 1:9). It also fits the circumstances of those who have suffered since for being followers of Jesus. John wanted those suffering for being followers of Jesus to read, hear, and take to heart what he was writing, "because the time is near" (Rev 1:3).

What was near to them? Perhaps the difficulties symbolized by the first five seals in Rev 6, as well as the spiritual warfare described in Rev 12 and 13.

What follows Rev 13:1–10 is a description of a second beast who forces people to bow down to an image of the first beast. These people are then marked to indicate their willingness to worship the first beast (vv. 11–18). This mark is called "the mark of the beast." What I've determined this mark to be, and the significance it has for Christians, will be the focus of the next chapter of this book.

This section of Revelation ends with a description of a harvest that takes place (Rev 14:15–20) following the coming of one seated on a cloud who is "like a son of man with a crown of gold on his head and a sharp sickle in his hand" (v. 14). As I noted previously, the one seated on the cloud is Jesus, and the harvest that takes place seems to be the same harvest described in the Parable of the Weeds.

Revelation 14:12 repeats an instruction in Rev 13:10 regarding how Christians are to respond when the events described in these chapters take place:

- "This calls for patient endurance and faithfulness on the part of God's people" (Rev 13:10).
- "This calls for patient endurance on the part of the people of God who keep his commands and remain faithful to Jesus" (Rev 14:12).

John was encouraging followers of Jesus to respond to the challenges that result from the war Satan has declared on Christians with patient endurance, by keeping God's commands no matter how hard it is to do at times, and by remaining faithful to Jesus no matter what difficulties or threats are faced.

SECTION 5: WHAT WILL EVENTUALLY HAPPEN TO JESUS' ENEMIES (REV 15-19)

The next five chapters of Revelation describe the time when God finally exercises his wrath against those who are enemies of him and Jesus. These chapters include descriptions of the following events:

- Seven angels appear with the last seven plagues. With these, God's wrath is completed (Rev 15:1).
- Seven bowls of wrath—the seven last plagues—are poured out upon the earth (Rev 16:1).
- Babylon, who may symbolize all who are or have been enemies of God, falls (Rev 18:1-3).
- A heavenly warrior—Jesus—defeats and condemns the beast and those who supported it (Rev 19:11-21).

Revelation 16:15 includes this instruction on what Christians are to do as the above unfolds:

> Look, I come like a thief! *Blessed is the one who stays awake and remains clothed*, so as not to go naked and be shamefully exposed.

As I noted in chapter 5, it appears from Rev 16:15 that followers of Jesus—those who have not already died physically—will still be alive on

Earth when the plagues described in Rev 15 and 16 are unleashed and the battles that follow commence.

What was revealed to John regarding the final battle between Jesus and his enemies (Rev 19:11–21) seems to be elaborating on what Paul said would precede the return of Jesus. I discussed this in chapter 4 when I compared John's description of this battle with one described in 2 Thess 2:1–4:

> 1 Concerning *the coming of our Lord Jesus Christ* and our being gathered to him, we ask you, brothers and sisters, 2 not to become easily unsettled or alarmed by the teaching allegedly from us— whether by a prophecy or by word of mouth or by letter—asserting that the day of the Lord has already come. 3 Don't let anyone deceive you in any way, for that day *will not come until the rebellion occurs and the man of lawlessness is revealed, the man doomed to destruction.* 4 He will oppose and will exalt himself over everything that is called God or is worshiped, so that he sets himself up in God's temple, proclaiming himself to be God.

As I noted when I discussed the above passage earlier, Paul said "the coming of our Lord" (v. 1) will not happen "until the rebellion occurs" (v. 3). It seems to me that the rebellion Paul was referring to in these verses is the same rebellion John described in Rev 19:11–21. This rebellion will culminate in a decisive battle between Jesus and forces aligned with Satan. Jesus will win this battle, resulting in the leaders arrayed against him being "thrown alive into the fiery lake of burning sulfur," and the rest of those fighting against Jesus killed (Rev 19:20–21).

Revelation is confirming that God's enemies will, in the end, receive the justice they deserve. In the meantime, followers of Jesus need to endure and remain faithful to Jesus. For though Christians are not destined to experience God's wrath, some will apparently be around when God's wrath is unleashed.

SECTION 6: WHAT WILL HAPPEN AFTER ALL OF THIS (REV 20–22)

The final chapters of Revelation begin with a description of these events:

- Satan is bound and thrown into the Abyss for a thousand years (Rev 20:1–3).

The Three Accounts of the Return of Jesus in Revelation

- Jesus reigns for a thousand years. Those who did not receive the mark of the beast reign with him (Rev 20:4–6).
- When the thousand years end, Satan is released for a time. But he is eventually thrown into the same lake of fire the beast was thrown into (Rev 20:7–11).
- Jesus sits on a white throne and judges the dead (Rev 20:11–15).

What I find significant about the above verses is that they depict a world quite different from the one we are living in today. It is a world where Satan has lost his influence and Jesus is reigning in person. Although we may find ourselves living in this world someday, we aren't living in it now. That may help to explain why Scripture includes few details regarding it.

Eventually all the terrible and challenging events described in Revelation will end. We will then live in a world that is new and perfect. In this world,

- There will be no more death, mourning, crying, or pain (Rev 21:4).
- A new Jerusalem will come down from heaven (Rev 21:9–14).
- Jesus will dwell in this city with us. We will worship and serve him (Rev 22:1–5).

There seems to be some conditions a person must meet, however, if they want to live in this new world:

- "Look, I am coming soon! *Blessed is the one who keeps the words of the prophecy written in this scroll*" (Rev 22:7).
- "Let the one who does right continue to *do right*; and let the holy person continue to *be holy*" (Rev 22:11c).
- "Look, I am coming soon! My reward is with me, and *I will give to each person according to what they have done*" (Rev 22:12).
- "*Blessed are those who wash their robes*, that they may have the right to the tree of life and may go through the gates into the city" (Rev 22:14).

Based on the verses above and ones discussed earlier, it seems to me that one must be in a saving relationship with Jesus, and have stayed in that relationship to the end of their life (or to the end of the age, whichever comes first), if they want to enjoy the benefits of the new world Jesus is going to create.

My conclusion about this is consistent with these instructions in Revelation:

- "Blessed is the one who reads aloud the words of this prophecy, and *blessed are those who hear it and take to heart what is written* in it, because the time is near" (Rev 1:3).
- "Whoever has ears, *let them hear what the Spirit says* to the churches" (Rev 2:7, 11, 17, and 29; 3:6, 13, and 22).
- "Do not be afraid of what you are about to suffer. . . . *Be faithful, even to the point of death*" (Rev 2:10).
- "*Repent*" (Rev 2:5, 16; 3:19).
- "*Wake up*" (Rev 3:2).
- "*Hold onto what you have*" (Rev 3:11).
- "*This calls for patient endurance and faithfulness* on the part of God's people" (Rev 13:10c; 14:12).
- "*This calls for wisdom*" (Rev 13:18).
- "*Blessed is the one who stays awake and remains clothed*, so as not to go naked and be shamefully exposed" (Rev 16:15).

The purpose of the above instructions is to bring to light how God wants Christians to respond when they face the challenges and difficulties described in Revelation.

Chapter 8

The Mark of the Beast

If anyone worships the beast and its image and receives its mark on their forehead or on their hand, they, too, will drink the wine of God's fury.

Revelation 14:9–10

As I've discussed why the Parable of the Weeds provides a credible framework for understanding other end-time passages in the Bible, I've emphasized how important it is, no matter what one believes about the end times, to always be found doing what is commendable in God's eyes. I've also pointed out how crucial it is that followers of Jesus remain faithful to Jesus to the end—that "the one who stands firm to the end will be saved" (Matt 24:13).

In this chapter, I will focus on what I consider to be one of the more important passages in the Bible regarding what can happen if a Christian does not remain faithful to Jesus and, at some point, denies knowing him. It is the description in Rev 13:11–18 of what some call "the mark of the beast":

> 11 Then I saw a second beast, coming out of the earth. It had two horns like a lamb, but it spoke like a dragon. 12 It exercised all the authority of the first beast on its behalf, and made the earth and its inhabitants worship the first beast, whose fatal wound had been healed. 13 And it performed great signs, even causing fire to come down from heaven to the earth in full view of the people. 14 Because of the signs it was given power to perform on behalf of the first beast, it deceived the inhabitants of the earth. It ordered them to set up an image in honor of the beast who was wounded

> by the sword and yet lived. 15 The second beast was given power to give breath to the image of the first beast, so that *the image could speak and cause all who refused to worship the image to be killed.* 16 It also forced all people, great and small, rich and poor, free and slave, to receive a mark on their right hands or on their foreheads, 17 *so that they could not buy or sell unless they had the mark, which is the name of the beast or the number of its name.*
>
> 18 This calls for wisdom. Let the person who has insight calculate the number of the beast, for it is the number of a man. That number is 666.

I won't describe here what the two beasts mentioned in Rev 13:11–18 seem to represent other than to note that they likely symbolize any individual or power closely aligned with Satan and what he is trying to accomplish. What I want to point out here is that the second beast gives breath to an image of the first, and that anyone who refuses to worship this image is killed (v. 15). The second beast also forces everyone to receive a mark on their right hand or forehead, perhaps as a sign of allegiance to the first beast, and that anyone who refuses to receive this mark is not allowed to buy or sell (v. 16).

It's this mark that people are referring to when talking about the mark of the beast.

There has been lots of speculation over the years regarding what the mark of the beast might be. Some have described it as some kind of physical indication that a person has given their loyalty to an individual or world power whose goal is to supplant Christ. A theory emerged at one time that it could be a global credit card that everyone would be required to carry if they wanted to buy or sell anything. Some have suggested the mark of the beast could be a microchip placed under a person's skin that identifies who they are and their medical history but also discloses personal information that is supposed to be private, including their religious affiliation. Some Christians feared it could be a nanobot introduced secretly into the bodies of those who agreed to be vaccinated during the recent COVID-19 pandemic.[3]

I used to agree with the traditional view that the mark of the beast will be a physical sign that a person has aligned themselves with the beast described in Rev 13. I had significant questions about this view, however. For one thing, if this mark will be something physical and so obviously associated with an evil power, why as a Christian would I bend my knees

---

3. Jimenez, "Mark of the Beast," secs. 4, 7, 9.

to this power by allowing myself to be marked by it? I also realized that if it will be something I might receive without knowing its connection to an anti-Christian world power, how could this possibly define me as one who is worshiping the beast? It didn't make sense that receiving this mark unknowingly could affect my relationship with God in any way.

These and other questions I had about the mark resulted in me looking more closely at Rev 13:11–18 and other related passages in order to get a better understanding of what John intended us to understand through these enigmatic verses.

The following sections summarize what I concluded as I did this.

IS THIS MARK LITERAL OR FIGURATIVE?

To understand what John was trying to convey in his description of the mark of the beast in Rev 13:11–18, one of the first steps is to determine if the mark he was describing was meant to be interpreted literally or figuratively. Will it be a physical mark? Or is its description meant to be understood as symbolic of something?

What's important to note when trying to answer these questions is that Revelation is heavily laced with symbolic language. Consider, for example, these images in Rev 13:

- A beast comes out of the sea. It has ten horns and seven heads (v. 1).
- This beast looks like a leopard but has feet of a bear and the mouth of a lion (v. 2).
- One of its heads has a fatal wound that has been healed (v. 3).
- A dragon, who symbolizes Satan (12:9), is worshiped because he gave authority to the beast (v. 4).
- The beast is given power to make war against the saints and to conquer them (v. 7).
- All whose names are not written in the book of life worship the beast (v. 8).
- Another beast comes out of the earth. It has two horns and speaks like a dragon (v. 11).
- The second beast has the same authority as the first (v. 12).
- The second beast sets up an image to honor the first beast (v. 14).

- This image is given breath. Those who refuse to worship it are killed (v. 15).
- No one can buy or sell unless they receive a mark on their right hand or forehead (vv. 16–17).
- This mark is the name of the beast or the number of its name (v. 17).
- The number of the beast is 666 (v. 18).

All of the above are symbolic. I don't expect, for example, that an actual beast with ten horns and seven heads will someday rise out of the sea and rule the world. This image symbolizes something—perhaps of powers, groups, or individuals who are enemies of Jesus and those who follow him.

The same can be said regarding the second beast. It is symbolic of a power or person who forces people to worship or give their allegiance to whatever the first beast represents, on the threat of physical or financial harm. But if these beasts are symbolic of someone or something, shouldn't the same conclusion be made regarding the mark associated with them? Shouldn't it be considered just as symbolic?

The issue here is to be consistent in how associated elements in Scripture are treated. I find it useful regarding these associations to apply a principle used in mathematics and logic called "the transitive law."[4] It can be stated as follows:

> If A is equal to B, and B is equal to C, then A is equal to C.

This is how this law could be stated when dealing with passages in the Bible that are predominantly symbolic:

> If element A in a passage is symbolic of something, and B is a characteristic of A, then B is symbolic of something as well.

This is how I would state this law in regard to the mark of the beast:

> Since the beast in this passage is symbolic of something, its mark is symbolic of something as well.

But if the mark of the beast is not a physical or literal marking but is symbolic of something, what is it symbolic of?

Answering that question requires a bit more digging.

---

4. Encyclopaedia Britannica, "Transitive Law," para. 1.

DOES THIS MARK SHOW UP ELSEWHERE IN SCRIPTURE?

As I noted earlier, one useful tool to help understand passages in the Bible that include symbolic images is to see if those images are found elsewhere in Scripture. When I looked into this, I found that Ezek 9:1–6 includes images similar to ones found in the description of the mark of the beast:

> 1 Then I heard him call out in a loud voice, "Bring near those who are appointed to execute judgment on the city, each with a weapon in his hand." 2 And I saw six men coming from the direction of the upper gate, which faces north, each with a deadly weapon in his hand. With them was a man clothed in linen who had a writing kit at his side. They came in and stood beside the bronze altar.
>
> 3 Now the glory of the God of Israel went up from above the cherubim, where it had been, and moved to the threshold of the temple. Then the LORD called to the man clothed in linen who had the writing kit at his side 4 and said to him, *"Go throughout the city of Jerusalem and put a mark on the foreheads of those who grieve and lament over all the detestable things that are done in it."*
>
> 5 As I listened, he said to the others, "Follow him through the city and kill, without showing pity or compassion. 6 Slaughter the old men, the young men and women, the mothers and children, *but do not touch anyone who has the mark*. Begin at my sanctuary." So they began with the old men who were in front of the temple.

Ezekiel was given this vision during the decline of Israel's relationship with God, prior to the destruction of Jerusalem by the Babylonians in 586 BC. One of the sins the Israelites were guilty of was idolatry (Ezek 8:1–3):

> 1 In the sixth year, in the sixth month on the fifth day, while I was sitting in my house and the elders of Judah were sitting before me, the hand of the Sovereign LORD came on me there. 2 I looked, and I saw a figure like that of a man. From what appeared to be his waist down he was like fire, and from there up his appearance was as bright as glowing metal. 3 He stretched out what looked like a hand and took me by the hair of my head. *The Spirit lifted me up between earth and heaven and in visions of God he took me to Jerusalem, to the entrance of the north gate of the inner court, where the idol that provokes to jealousy stood.*

In addition to worshiping idols, Israel's religious leaders were guilty of other detestable things, including bowing down to the sun in the east (Ezek 8:7–16):

> 7 Then he brought me to the entrance to the court. I looked, and I saw a hole in the wall. 8 He said to me, "Son of man, now dig into the wall." So I dug into the wall and saw a doorway there.
>
> 9 And he said to me, *"Go in and see the wicked and detestable things they are doing here."* 10 So I went in and looked, and I saw portrayed all over the walls all kinds of crawling things and unclean animals and all the idols of Israel. 11 In front of them stood seventy elders of Israel, and Jaazaniah son of Shaphan was standing among them. Each had a censer in his hand, and a fragrant cloud of incense was rising.
>
> 12 He said to me, *"Son of man, have you seen what the elders of Israel are doing in the darkness, each at the shrine of his own idol? They say, 'The Lord does not see us; the Lord has forsaken the land.'"* 13 Again, he said, "You will see them doing things that are even more detestable."
>
> 14 Then he brought me to the entrance of the north gate of the house of the Lord, and I saw women sitting there, mourning the god Tammuz. 15 He said to me, *"Do you see this, son of man? You will see things that are even more detestable than this."*
>
> 16 He then brought me into the inner court of the house of the Lord, and there at the entrance to the temple, between the portico and the altar, were about twenty-five men. With their backs toward the temple of the Lord and their faces toward the east, *they were bowing down to the sun in the east.*

The elders thought that God didn't know what they were doing (v. 12). But he did.

This is how God responded (Ezek 8:17–18):

> 17 He said to me, "Have you seen this, son of man? Is it a trivial matter for the people of Judah to do the detestable things they are doing here? Must they also fill the land with violence and continually arouse my anger? Look at them putting the branch to their nose! 18 Therefore *I will deal with them in anger*; I will not look on them with pity or spare them. Although they shout in my ears, *I will not listen to them."*

God was angry. He told the Israelites that he was no longer going to listen to them; he was no longer going to hear their prayers; he was no longer going to protect them from their enemies.

Ezekiel 9:1–6 describes in symbolic language what God intended to do in response to his anger over the Israelites' detestable practices:

- Six men with deadly weapons would be appointed to execute judgment on the city (vv. 1–2a).
- They would be joined by a man dressed in linen carrying a writing kit (v. 2b).
- The man in linen would mark the foreheads of those who grieved over Israel's idolatry (vv. 3–4).
- Those unmarked would be killed by the six (vv. 5–6).

There is nothing in Ezekiel 9:1–6 that compels one to conclude that the marking occurred just as described. Although many Jews died when the Babylonians destroyed Jerusalem, there is no evidence here or elsewhere in Scripture that anyone literally walked through the streets of Jerusalem prior to its destruction, physically marking those who were to be spared. The marking that took place, one I like to call "the mark of the angel," is best understood as a *demarcation* and not a physical marking. In the context of the time and circumstances, this demarcation was a separation in the eyes of God between those who were faithful to him and those who were not—between those who grieved and lamented over all the detestable things done by the Israelites (Ezek 9:4), and those who did not.

Here are parallels I've found between the marking described in Ezek 9:1–6 and the mark of the beast:

- The primary issue is the worship of idols.
- A marking takes place based on the response to this.
- One place where people are marked is on their forehead.
- There are significant consequences for those marked, as well as those who aren't.

What's different between the two passages is who is marked and who is not. In Ezek 9:1–6, the ones marked were those who lamented and grieved "over all the detestable things" that were being done (v. 4). In Rev 13:11–18, the ones marked will be those who choose to identify with the beast, lest they lose their ability to buy and sell (vv. 16–17).

There is also a difference in who is judged. Regarding the mark of the angel, it is those who were unmarked. Regarding the mark of the beast, as these verses note, it is those who are marked (Rev 14:9–10):

> 9 A third angel followed them and said in a loud voice: "*If anyone worships the beast and its image and receives its mark on their forehead or on their hand,* 10 *they, too, will drink the wine of God's fury, which has been poured full strength into the cup of his wrath. They will be tormented with burning sulfur in the presence of the holy angels and of the Lamb.*"

What Rev 14:9–10 doesn't explicitly identify is whom John was concerned about when he wrote that "*they, too,* [those who worship the beast and receive its mark] *will drink the wine of God's fury*" (v. 10). It certainly can't be unbelievers—those who are not followers of Jesus. The fate of unbelievers will be set based on their rejection of Jesus, not by their decision to allow themselves to be marked by a person or power aligned with Satan.

I've concluded that the only ones who can be affected by this demarcation—by the mark of the beast—are Christians. If this is so, then this mark is a concern *only* for Christians.

When I discussed my understanding of chapters 12 through 14 of Revelation in chapter 7 of this book, I noted that there are spiritual forces in this world aligned with Satan and his goal to supplant Christ. One goal of Satan and these evil forces is to keep those separated from God from having a saving relationship with Jesus.

These dark forces are attacking Christians as well. One of the goals of these forces is to silence those already in a relationship with Jesus. But they also want to put Christians in situations that could result in them falling away from their faith or in denying that they know Jesus. One weapon Satan and these evil forces use in their attempts to accomplish this are threats of physical or financial harm—by making it difficult for those unwilling to give their allegiance to them to buy or sell (Rev 13:17).

It seems to me that the mark of the beast is something a Christian does to avoid the suffering these dark powers threaten to subject them to for being a follower of Christ.

What might this mark—this demarcation—be? In the first and second centuries, it could have been a Christian who denied they were a follower of Jesus in order to be spared from the jaws of lions in a Roman arena or from death by sword of a pagan soldier.

One example of someone who refused to be marked this way was Polycarp, Bishop of the church in Smyrna in the second century. Around AD 160, at the age of eighty-six, Polycarp was arrested by the Romans and threatened with execution if he didn't reproach Christ.[5] He refused to do so and, shortly afterward, was executed by the Romans.[6]

For Polycarp, the beast was Rome, and the mark would have been reproaching Jesus, perhaps by distancing himself from Jesus or rebuking Jesus, in order to avoid being executed.

Today, the mark of the beast could be something a Christian does to avoid being killed, imprisoned, or financially harmed for being a follower of Jesus. This could include worshiping some other god, or pretending to, in order to avoid being persecuted for declaring that Jesus alone is Lord. It could also include denying that one is a follower of Jesus in order to avoid being harmed for identifying with him.

There are significant and potentially eternal consequences for Christians who make this type of accommodation to individuals or powers aligned with Satan, something the next section will point out.

WHAT ARE THE CONSEQUENCES OF BEING MARKED?

Revelation 14:6–12 includes a description of what happens to those marked by the beast:

> 6 Then I saw another angel flying in midair, and he had the eternal gospel to proclaim to those who live on the earth—to every nation, tribe, language and people. 7 He said in a loud voice, "Fear God and give him glory, because the hour of his judgment has come. Worship him who made the heavens, the earth, the sea and the springs of water."
>
> 8 A second angel followed and said, "'Fallen! Fallen is Babylon the Great,' which made all the nations drink the maddening wine of her adulteries."
>
> 9 A third angel followed them and said in a loud voice: *"If anyone worships the beast and its image and receives its mark on their forehead or on their hand, 10 they, too, will drink the wine of God's fury,* which has been poured full strength into the cup of his wrath. They will be tormented with burning sulfur in the presence of the holy angels and of the Lamb. 11 And the smoke of their torment

---

5. Polycarp responded, "86 years have I have served him, and he has done me no wrong. How can I blaspheme my King and my Savior?" Christian History Institute, "Polycarp's Martyrdom," para. 1.

6. Christian History Institute, "Polycarp's Martyrdom," sects. 9, 15–16. The Romans tried to burn Polycarp on a pile of wood. When this miraculously failed, they pierced him with a dagger.

will rise for ever and ever. There will be no rest day or night for those who worship the beast and its image, or for anyone who receives the mark of its name." 12 This calls for patient endurance on the part of the people of God who keep his commands and remain faithful to Jesus.

There appears to be three groups of people in the above passage. There are those who drink the maddening wine of the adulteries of "Babylon the Great" (v. 8); there are those who do not drink this wine but who nevertheless worship the beast and receive its mark (v. 9–10); and there are those who remain faithful to Jesus (v. 12).

The first of these three groups are unbelievers—those who, when given the opportunity to follow Jesus, don't "fear God and give him the glory," and don't "worship him who made the heavens, the earth, the sea and the springs of water" (v. 7).

The third group are those who fear God and worship him and remain faithful to Jesus to the end (v. 12).

Who, then, is among those included in the second group?

It seems to me that it is Christians who do not remain faithful to Jesus in the midst of suffering or persecution or, in response to economic or physical threats, deny knowing Jesus.

What will the fate be of those who were once followers of Jesus but who end up marked for disowning him? If they are the "they, too" Rev 14:10 is referring to, then *"they, too . . . will be tormented with burning sulfur in the presence of the holy angels and of the Lamb."*

Revelation 21:6–8 seems to include similar groups of people:

> 6 He said to me: "It is done. I am the Alpha and the Omega, the Beginning and the End. To the thirsty I will give water without cost from the spring of the water of life. 7 *Those who are victorious* will inherit all this, and I will be their God and they will be my children. 8 But the cowardly, *the unbelieving*, the vile, the murderers, the sexually immoral, those who practice magic arts, the idolaters and all liars—they will be consigned to the fiery lake of burning sulfur. This is the second death."

Although Rev 21:6–8 seems to be describing numerous groups of people, they can be put into the same three found in Rev 14:6–12.

The first are those "who are victorious" (v. 7). This most likely is referring to Christians who persevere in the midst of trials—those who do not cave into the world system or deny knowing Jesus in order to avoid suffering.

The second are "the unbelieving" (v. 8). This seems to be referring to those who have never made a commitment to follow Jesus.

Who then is in the third group, one that includes cowards, murderers, liars, those who are sexually immoral, and the like (v. 8)? It cannot be referring to unbelievers—those who have never made a commitment to follow Jesus. That's because the fate of unbelievers is sealed by their unbelief, not by the nature or extent of their sin. This third group must therefore be those who call themselves followers of Jesus but live as if they aren't.

John wrote that there are dreadful consequences for those in this third group. Along with the unbelieving, "they will be consigned to the fiery lake of burning sulfur" (v. 8).

The warnings in the above passages are similar to ones recorded elsewhere in Scripture. Jesus, for example, issued this warning in Matt 10:32–33:

> 32 *Whoever acknowledges me* before others, I will also acknowledge before my Father in heaven. 33 *But whoever disowns* me before others, I will disown before my Father in heaven.

Paul issued a similar warning in 2 Tim 2:12:

> *If we endure,*
>   we will also reign with him.
> *If we disown him,*
>   he will also disown us.

The necessity of enduring and remaining faithful to Jesus in the midst of pressures to disown him was something John emphasized often in Revelation. Revelation 13:9–10, for example, notes what John wrote following his description of the war Satan has declared on Christians:

> 9 Whoever has ears, let them hear.
> 10 "If anyone is to go into captivity,
>   into captivity they will go.
> If anyone is to be killed with the sword,
>   with the sword they will be killed."
> *This calls for patient endurance and faithfulness on the part of God's people.*

The phrase highlighted above is nearly identical to the one highlighted below in Rev 14:12. It follows John's description of the consequences of allowing oneself to be marked by the beast:

> *This calls for patient endurance on the part of the people of God* who keep his commands and remain faithful to Jesus.

It seems from the above that God is urging followers of Jesus to endure the suffering Satan and his minions are instigating in the hope that they can get Christians to abandon their faith. If those who have made a commitment to follow Jesus don't endure to the end—if at some point, a Christian denies they know Jesus or refuses to identify with him—I believe they risk experiencing the same fate of those who have never been followers of Jesus.

I discussed Matt 24:9–13 previously, but it is worth repeating:

> 9 Then you will be handed over to be persecuted and put to death, and you will be hated by all nations because of me. 10 At that time many will turn away from the faith and will betray and hate each other, 11 and many false prophets will appear and deceive many people. 12 Because of the increase of wickedness, the love of most will grow cold, 13 *but the one who stands firm to the end will be saved.*

Jesus told his disciples that identifying with him and defending the gospel message was not going to be easy. Those who followed him would be hated. Some would be persecuted and some betrayed, and some would be put to death. Some who followed Jesus would abandon their faith in order to avoid suffering for being a follower of Jesus.

Jesus promised that those who stand firm to the end will be saved (Matt 24:13). Implied with this is a warning that those who do not stand firm to the end will not be saved. Could this be the same message John was trying to convey through his description of the beast and the consequences of allowing oneself to be marked by it?

It seems to me that it is the same message.

John was warning that there are terrible consequences for those who claim to be followers of Jesus but who try to avoid suffering by compromising with world powers opposed to Jesus, who deny they are followers of Jesus in order to protect their physical or financial well-being, or who drink the maddening wine of the world's adulteries.

In chapter 5 of this book, when noting passages in the Bible that compare the return of Jesus with the coming a thief, I mentioned this passage in 2 Pet 3:10–18:

> 10 But the day of the Lord will come like a thief. The heavens will disappear with a roar; the elements will be destroyed by fire, and the earth and everything done in it will be laid bare.
>
> 11 Since everything will be destroyed in this way, what kind of people ought you to be? *You ought to live holy and godly lives* 12 as you look forward to the day of God and speed its coming. That day will bring about the destruction of the heavens by fire, and the elements will melt in the heat. 13 But in keeping with his promise we are looking forward to a new heaven and a new earth, where righteousness dwells.
>
> 14 So then, dear friends, since you are looking forward to this, *make every effort to be found spotless, blameless and at peace with him.* 15 Bear in mind that our Lord's patience means salvation, just as our dear brother Paul also wrote you with the wisdom that God gave him. 16 *He writes the same way* in all his letters, speaking in them of these matters. His letters contain some things that are hard to understand, *which ignorant and unstable people distort*, as they do the other Scriptures, *to their own destruction.*
>
> 17 Therefore, dear friends, since you have been forewarned, *be on your guard so that you may not be carried away by the error of the lawless and fall from your secure position.* 18 But grow in the grace and knowledge of our Lord and Savior Jesus Christ. To him be glory both now and forever! Amen.

Peter told his audience that, as they waited for the return of Jesus, they were to "live holy and godly lives" (v. 11) and "be found spotless, blameless and at peace with him" (v. 14). Peter warned that some would distort what he and Paul were teaching about this and the return of Jesus (v. 16). He urged followers of Jesus to be on their guard lest they be carried away by the error of lawless men and fall from their secure position (v. 17).

Was Peter warning that a Christian can fall away from their secure position once they've come into a saving relationship with Jesus?

Apparently so.

What could cause this to happen?

Perhaps it is by listening to those who say that, once you've become a Christian, it no longer matters how you live.

Perhaps it is by listening to those who say it's alright to hide what you believe about Jesus if sharing your faith would result in being ostracized by those who don't believe in him.

Perhaps it is by denying that one is a follower of Jesus in order to protect one's physical or financial well-being.

Christians, Unpack Your Bags!

What are the consequences of doing so?

Perhaps it is to share the fate of those who don't know Jesus at all.

And so, if you are a Christian and are tempted to deny that you know Jesus, or if you are a follower of Jesus and are tempted to live like those who don't know Jesus at all, my advice is this: *don't do it*! For if my understanding of the passages discussed in this chapter is correct, the consequences of doing so will be dire.

Chapter 9

Antichrists, Beasts, Tribulation, and the Last Days

> *Dear children, this is the last hour; and as you have heard that the antichrist is coming, even now many antichrists have come. This is how we know it is the last hour.*
>
> 1 John 2:18

As I used the framework of the Parable of the Weeds to help understand other end-time passages, I came across phrases utilized when describing the end times that I felt warranted more exploration. In this and the following chapter, I will discuss what I learned as I looked into these.

ANTICHRISTS

I remember sitting with a friend at a restaurant a while back who had a strong "pre-tribulation rapture" mindset regarding the end times. As we were discussing the character of the world and her view that conditions were rapidly sinking into a state of moral chaos, she asked, "Do you think the Antichrist is already here?" What I think she meant by this is, "Do you think the leader Revelation says will rule in the seven-year period following the rapture of the church is here?" I gave her a quick but short answer, "Yes, I believe he is already here," then changed the subject, knowing that her understanding of who or what the antichrist may be was significantly different than mine.

I'd already discovered by then that there are only four verses in the Bible that include the word "antichrist." Here are those four:

- "Dear children, this is the last hour; and as you have heard that *the antichrist is coming, even now many antichrists have come.* This is how we know it is the last hour" (1 John 2:18).
- "Who is the liar? It is *whoever denies that Jesus is the Christ. Such a person is the antichrist*—denying the Father and the Son. 23 No one who denies the Son has the Father; whoever acknowledges the Son has the Father also" (1 John 2:22-23).
- "*But every spirit that does not acknowledge Jesus is not from God. This is the spirit of the antichrist*, which you have heard is coming and even now is already in the world" (1 John 4:3).
- "I say this because many deceivers, who do not acknowledge Jesus Christ as coming in the flesh, have gone out into the world. *Any such person is the deceiver and the antichrist*" (2 John 1:7).

What the verses above have in common is that they don't describe the antichrist as a single individual. Instead, they describe the antichrist as *anyone* who "denies that Jesus is the Christ" (1 John 2:22). From the perspective of John and those he was writing to, many antichrists had already come, and more were on the horizon (1 John 2:18).

The apostle Paul was an antichrist before he met Jesus on the road to Damascus and became a follower of Jesus (Acts 8:1-3). So was everyone else in the first century who tried to prevent the dissemination of the gospel message, including those who threatened to kill, torture, or imprison anyone who embraced it.

Over the centuries, there have been innumerable people who have opposed the propagation of the gospel message or the proclamation that Jesus is the Son of God. Some of them have done great harm to those who are committed followers of Jesus. All are, or were, antichrists.

That doesn't mean there won't be an individual antichrist who rises to power as we get closer to the end of the age. The point here is that the Bible doesn't treat the antichrist as a single person or power. The antichrist is anyone who has opposed, or currently opposes, the proclamation that Jesus is the Son of God.

Antichrists, Beasts, Tribulation, and the Last Days

BEASTS

In chapter 7, I shared some thoughts about what the beast described in Rev 13 may be. I will now compare this beast with those described in Rev 17 and Dan 7.

This is how Rev 13:1–8 describes this beast:

> 1 The dragon stood on the shore of the sea. And *I saw a beast coming out of the sea. It had ten horns and seven heads*, with ten crowns on its horns, and on each head a blasphemous name. 2 The beast I saw resembled a leopard, but had feet like those of a bear and a mouth like that of a lion. The dragon gave the beast his power and his throne and great authority. 3 One of the heads of the beast seemed to have had a fatal wound, but the fatal wound had been healed. The whole world was filled with wonder and followed the beast. 4 People worshiped the dragon because he had given authority to the beast, and they also worshiped the beast and asked, "Who is like the beast? Who can wage war against it?"
>
> 5 The beast was given a mouth to utter proud words and blasphemies and to exercise its authority for forty-two months. 6 It opened its mouth to blaspheme God, and to slander his name and his dwelling place and those who live in heaven. 7 *It was given power to wage war against God's holy people and to conquer them.* And *it was given authority over every tribe, people, language and nation.* 8 All inhabitants of the earth will worship the beast—all whose names have not been written in the Lamb's book of life, the Lamb who was slain from the creation of the world.

This is how Rev 17:6–14 describes this beast:

> 6 I saw that the woman was drunk with the blood of God's holy people, the blood of those who bore testimony to Jesus.
>
> I saw her, I was greatly astonished. 7 Then the angel said to me: "Why are you astonished? I will explain to you the mystery of the woman and of *the beast* she rides, *which has the seven heads and ten horns.* 8 *The beast, which you saw, once was, now is not, and yet will come* up out of the Abyss and go to its destruction. The inhabitants of the earth whose names have not been written in the book of life from the creation of the world will be astonished when they see the beast, *because it once was, now is not, and yet will come.*
>
> 9 "This calls for a mind with wisdom. *The seven heads* are seven hills on which the woman sits. 10 They *are also seven kings. Five have fallen, one is, the other has not yet come*; but when he does come, he must remain for only a little while. 11 The beast who

> once was, and now is not, is an eighth king. He belongs to the seven and is going to his destruction.
>
> 12 *"The ten horns you saw are ten kings who have not yet received a kingdom, but who for one hour will receive authority as kings along with the beast.* 13 They have one purpose and will give their power and authority to the beast. 14 They will wage war against the Lamb, but the Lamb will triumph over them because he is Lord of lords and King of kings—and with him will be his called, chosen and faithful followers."

Since the beast in Rev 13 and the one in Rev 17 are both described as having ten horns and seven heads, they are most likely the same beast.

Some may maintain, however, that these passages are describing two different beasts, especially if they view chapters 4 through 19 of Revelation as a chronological description of end-time events. But as I noted in chapter 7 of this book, I've concluded there are three different accounts of the return of Jesus in Revelation. If this is so, then the description of the beast in Rev 13 is in the section of Revelation that includes the second account of Jesus' return (chapters 12 through 14), while its description in Rev 17 is in the section of Revelation that includes the third account of Jesus' return (chapters 15 through 19).

Daniel was also given a vision of a beast. The beast Daniel saw in his vision (Dan 7:7-8) is similar to the beasts described in both Rev 13 and 17:

> 7 After that, in my vision at night I looked, and there before me was a fourth beast—terrifying and frightening and very powerful. It had large iron teeth; *it crushed and devoured its victims* and trampled underfoot whatever was left. It was different from all the former beasts, and *it had ten horns.*
>
> 8 While I was thinking about the horns, there before me was another horn, a little one, which came up among them; and three of the first horns were uprooted before it. This horn had eyes like the eyes of a human being and a mouth that spoke boastfully.

Daniel 7:19-25 records what this beast symbolizes:

> 19 Then I wanted to know the meaning of the fourth beast, which was different from all the others and most terrifying, with its iron teeth and bronze claws—the beast that crushed and devoured its victims and trampled underfoot whatever was left. 20 I also wanted to know about the ten horns on its head and about the other horn that came up, before which three of them fell—the horn that looked more imposing than the others and that had eyes

> and a mouth that spoke boastfully. 21 As I watched, *this horn was waging war against the holy people and defeating them, 22 until the Ancient of Days came and pronounced judgment in favor of the holy people of the Most High, and the time came when they possessed the kingdom.*
>
> 23 He gave me this explanation: "The fourth beast is a fourth kingdom that will appear on earth. It will be different from all the other kingdoms and will devour the whole earth, trampling it down and crushing it. 24 *The ten horns are ten kings* who will come from this kingdom. After them another king will arise, different from the earlier ones; he will subdue three kings. 25 *He will speak against the Most High and oppress his holy people* and try to change the set times and the laws. *The holy people will be delivered into his hands* for a time, times and half a time."

Here are similarities in how the beasts in Rev 13 and 17, and the one Dan 7, are described:

- The beast has ten horns (Rev 13:1 and 17:7; Dan 7:7).
- The ten horns symbolize ten kings that haven't yet come (Rev 17:12; Dan 7:24).
- The beast wages war against God's holy people (Rev 13:7; Dan 7:21, 25).
- This war won't end until Jesus—the "Ancient of Days"—comes (Rev 17:14; Dan 7:22).

Based on these similarities, it seems that all three passages are describing the same beast.

Regarding the ten horns, they symbolize ten kings that from both Daniel's and John's perspectives were in the future (Dan 7:24; Rev 17:12). Though these ten kings could still be in our future, nothing in the context of Revelation precludes that some of these kings may have already come and gone.

The beast's seven heads, something only the passages in Revelation mention, symbolize seven kings (Rev 17:9–11). From John's perspective, five of these kings were in the past, one existed then, and one was in his future.

From Daniel's perspective, the beast was in the future (Dan 7:23). From John's perspective, it existed in the past, didn't exist then, but would come to power again sometime in the future (Rev 17:8).

Although some may interpret separately what the horns, heads, and the beast itself symbolize, I am inclined to consider the image as a whole without getting too bogged down in the details of it.

The image of a beast with ten horns and seven heads could symbolize that opposition to Jesus and those who follow him will come in many different forms and varying levels of intensity. The beast could be any individual or power—past, present, or future—who aligns with Satan and his goal to keep people separated from God, silence those already in a relationship with Jesus, or cause those who follow Jesus to fall away from their faith.

THE GREAT TRIBULATION

One event I've often heard those who believe in a pre-tribulation rapture discuss is "the Great Tribulation." What some understand this to be is the seven-year period of suffering and judgment the world will experience following the rapture of the church.

The phrase, "the great tribulation," does show up in Rev 7:9–14:

> 9 After this I looked, and there before me was a great multitude that no one could count, from every nation, tribe, people and language, standing before the throne and before the Lamb. They were wearing white robes and were holding palm branches in their hands. 10 And they cried out in a loud voice:
> "Salvation belongs to our God,
> who sits on the throne,
> and to the Lamb."
> 11 All the angels were standing around the throne and around the elders and the four living creatures. They fell down on their faces before the throne and worshiped God, 12 saying:
> "Amen!
> Praise and glory
> and wisdom and thanks and honor
> and power and strength
> be to our God for ever and ever.
> Amen!"
> 13 Then one of the elders asked me, "These in white robes—who are they, and where did they come from?"
> 14 I answered, "Sir, you know."
> And he said, *"These are they who have come out of the great tribulation; they have washed their robes and made them* white in the blood of the Lamb."

What did those speaking in this verse mean when they used the phrase, "the great tribulation" (v. 14)? Were they referring to, for example, a fixed period of increasing difficulties the entire world will be subjected to prior to the moment when Jesus returns to judge the wicked and reward the righteous? Or were they referring to challenges and suffering all Christians were destined to experience, beginning in the first century?

What is interesting is that the Greek word translated "tribulation" in Rev 7:14, *thlipsis*, is translated a number of ways in the New Testament. This includes

- persecuted (Matt 24:9)
- distress (Matt 24:21, 29; Mark 13:19, 24)
- trouble (John 16:33; Rom 2:9, 8:35)
- suffering (Rom 5:3; 1 Thess 1:6; Rev 1:9, 2:10, 22)
- affliction (Rom 12:12; Rev 2:9)
- tribulation (Rev 7:14)

After noting ways *thlipsis* is translated, I don't get the sense it is referring to a fixed period of time in the future when unbelievers will be subjected to an intense period of trials and judgment. *Thlipsis* seems to be describing the persecution, distress, troubles, suffering, afflictions, and tribulation Christians will experience no matter what times or places they are living in. Some of the difficulties Christians experience will be the result of their commitment to be followers of Jesus. But some of these difficulties will be hardships common to all who, according to the Parable of the Weeds, will be living in the same field until the harvest at the end of the age.

This understanding of what tribulation means may be what Jesus had in mind when he said this (John 16:33):

> I have told you these things, so that in me you may have peace. In this world you will have *trouble* [*thlipsis*]. But take heart! I have overcome the world.

Jesus was telling his disciples that they were going to experience a significant amount of *thlipsis* in their lifetime.

When Paul wrote his first letter to the church in Thessalonica, it seems that Christians there were already experiencing *thlipsis* (1 Thess 1:6):

> You became imitators of us and of the Lord, for you welcomed the message in the midst of severe *suffering* [*thlipsis*] with the joy given by the Holy Spirit.

Those John was writing to were experiencing *thlipsis* as well (Rev 1:9):

> I, John, your brother and companion in the *suffering* [*thlipsis*] and kingdom and patient endurance that are ours in Jesus, was on the island of Patmos because of the word of God and the testimony of Jesus.

But if tribulation is meant to be understood in general as the ongoing suffering and afflictions Christians will experience prior to the return of Jesus, what is Rev 7:14 referring to when it says, "These are they who have come out of *the great tribulation*; they have washed their robes and made them white in the blood of the Lamb"?

One help in answering this is to note where else the image of Christians "wearing white robes" (Rev 7:9) shows up in Scripture. Revelation 6:9–11 is one of them:

> 9 When he opened the fifth seal, I saw under the altar the souls of those who had been slain because of the word of God and the testimony they had maintained. 10 They called out in a loud voice, "How long, Sovereign Lord, holy and true, until you judge the inhabitants of the earth and avenge our blood?" 11 *Then each of them was given a white robe, and they were told to wait a little longer,* until the full number of their fellow servants, their brothers and sisters, were killed just as they had been.

As I noted in chapter 7, the first four seals in Revelation 6 describe challenges that will affect everyone. The fifth seal, however, describes challenges reserved only for Christians. It is the persecution Christians will be subjected to for being followers of Jesus. In John's vision, those killed (v. 9) want to know when this period of persecution is going to end and those instigating it judged (v. 10).

What was Jesus' answer?

"Wait a little longer" (v. 11).

When did this period of persecution begin? I believe it began in the first century when Satan failed to keep Jesus in the grave and in anger, "went off to wage war against the rest of her offspring—those who keep God's commands and hold fast their testimony about Jesus" (Rev 12:17). As a result of this war, some Christians will be taken captive, and some will be killed (Rev 13:10). Some will apparently allow themselves to be marked by the Beast in order to avoid financial or physical harm for being a follower of Jesus (Rev 13:11–18).

Based on my understanding of the passages discussed in this section, it's my conclusion that the period John called "the great tribulation" began in the first century. If this is so, then Christians have been living in a period of great *thlipsis* for nearly two thousand years and are living in it still today.

THE LAST DAYS

Another term commonly heard when discussing the end times is "the last days." In the New Testament, it has two different meanings. One of these is in Acts 2:14–21:

> 14 Then Peter stood up with the Eleven, raised his voice and addressed the crowd: "Fellow Jews and all of you who live in Jerusalem, let me explain this to you; listen carefully to what I say. 15 These people are not drunk, as you suppose. It's only nine in the morning! 16 No, this is what was spoken by the prophet Joel:
> 17 '*In the last days, God says,*
> *I will pour out my Spirit on all people.*
> Your sons and daughters will prophesy,
>   your young men will see visions,
>   your old men will dream dreams.
> 18 Even on my servants, both men and women,
>   I will pour out my Spirit in those days,
>   and they will prophesy.
> 19 I will show wonders in the heavens above
>   and signs on the earth below,
>   blood and fire and billows of smoke.
> 20 The sun will be turned to darkness
>   and the moon to blood
>   before the coming of the great and glorious day of the Lord.
> 21 And everyone who calls
>   on the name of the Lord will be saved.'"

Much of what Peter expressed in the above comes from Joel 2:28–32:

> 28 And afterward,
>   I will pour out my Spirit on all people.
> Your sons and daughters will prophesy,
>   your old men will dream dreams,
>   your young men will see visions.

> 29 Even on my servants, both men and women,
>   I will pour out my Spirit in those days.
> 30 I will show wonders in the heavens
>   and on the earth,
>   blood and fire and billows of smoke.
> 31 The sun will be turned to darkness
>   and the moon to blood
>   before the coming of the great and dreadful day of the Lord.
> 32 And everyone who calls
>   on the name of the Lord will be saved;
> for on Mount Zion and in Jerusalem
>   there will be deliverance,
>   as the Lord has said,
> even among the survivors
>   whom the Lord calls.

Peter voiced what is recorded in Acts 2:14–21 shortly after he and the other remaining disciples received the gift of the Holy Spirit and began speaking in tongues (Acts 2:1–13). This occurred in Jerusalem on the day of Pentecost following Jesus' resurrection. Some of those observing this thought that Jesus' disciples were drunk. Peter responded by stating that what the Jews were witnessing was the fulfillment of a prophecy in Joel that in the last days, God was going to pour out his spirit on all people (Joel 2:28–29).

Peter's use of the phrase "the last days" in Acts 2:17 can't be understood in any other way than that Peter thought he and those he was speaking to were living in the last days.

This understanding of what "the last days" means seems to be the intent of its use in Heb 1:1–2 as well:

> 1 In the past God spoke to our ancestors through the prophets at many times and in various ways, 2 *but in these last days he has spoken to us by his Son*, whom he appointed heir of all things, and through whom also he made the universe.

A phrase similar to "the last days"—"the last hour"—is found in 1 John 2:18:

> Dear children, *this is the last hour*; and as you have heard that the antichrist is coming, even now many antichrists have come. This is how we know *it is the last hour*.

It is apparent from reading the above that John thought that he and those he was writing to were already living in the last hour.

There are other passages where "the last days" could be referring to a future time, however. Second Timothy 3:1–5 is one of them:

> 1 But mark this: *There will be terrible times in the last days.* 2 People will be lovers of themselves, lovers of money, boastful, proud, abusive, disobedient to their parents, ungrateful, unholy, 3 without love, unforgiving, slanderous, without self-control, brutal, not lovers of the good, 4 treacherous, rash, conceited, lovers of pleasure rather than lovers of God— 5 having a form of godliness but denying its power. Have nothing to do with such people.

Although Paul's use of the phrase "the last days" in the above passage could be referring to conditions that were occurring at that time or to conditions that were right around the corner, it seems more likely that Paul was describing conditions that wouldn't occur until sometime in the distant future.

I've concluded that "the last days" should be understood in general as starting sometime early in the first century, beginning perhaps when Jesus was baptized, but certainly starting no later than the celebration of Pentecost that followed Jesus' resurrection. In some contexts, however, "the last days" could be describing conditions that will not exist until the world is closer to the end of the age.

Christians in the first century were living in the last days. We are as well. But some conditions the Bible says will characterize the last days may still be ahead.

Chapter 10

The Bride of Christ and the Pre-Wrath Rapture

> *As a young man marries a young woman,*
> *so will your Builder marry you;*
> *as a bridegroom rejoices over his bride,*
> *so will your God rejoice over you.*
>
> ISAIAH 62:5

ONE PHRASE I OFTEN hear when discussing views about the end times is "the bride of Christ."

Some Christians believe the church—all who have entered into a saving relationship with Jesus—is the bride of Christ. And some believe that Jesus' bride will be gathered to be with Jesus—in fact, *must* be gathered to Jesus—prior to a seven-year period of trials, tribulation, and judgment for those left behind.

What caused me to question if the church is the bride of Christ are these passages in Revelation:

- 1 "Then I saw 'a new heaven and a new earth,' for the first heaven and the first earth had passed away, and there was no longer any sea. 2 *I saw the Holy City, the new Jerusalem, coming down out of heaven from God, prepared as a bride beautifully dressed for her husband.* 3 And I heard a loud voice from the throne saying, 'Look! God's dwelling place is now among the people, and he will dwell with them. They will be his people, and God himself will be with them and be their God. 4 He will wipe every tear from their eyes. There will be no more death' or

- 9 "One of the seven angels who had the seven bowls full of the seven last plagues came and said to me, '*Come, I will show you the bride, the wife of Lamb.*' 10 *And he carried me away in the Spirit to a mountain great and high, and showed me the Holy City, Jerusalem, coming down out of heaven from God.* 11 It shone with the glory of God, and its brilliance was like that of a very precious jewel, like a jasper, clear as crystal. 12 It had a great, high wall with twelve gates, and with twelve angels at the gates. On the gates were written the names of the twelve tribes of Israel. 13 There were three gates on the east, three on the north, three on the south and three on the west. 14 The wall of the city had twelve foundations, and on them were the names of the twelve apostles of the Lamb" (Rev 21:9–14).

What strikes me about the verses above is how un-church-like they are. For the most part, they include images more commonly associated with the Jews—with Israel—than with the church. For example:

- Jerusalem (v. 2) was the capital of the Jewish nation. It was also the city where the temple was built so that God could dwell in the midst of his people.
- The names written on its gates (v. 12) are the names of the twelve tribes of Israel.
- Although the twelve apostles whose names are written on the foundations of the wall (v. 14) were among the early leaders of the church, all twelve were Jews.
- Nothing in these verses explicitly references the church.

Revelation 21:1–4 and 21:9–14 both indicate that the bride of Christ is Jerusalem. But who or what does Jerusalem symbolize? Is it the church? Or could it be someone or something else?

DOES JESUS HAVE A BRIDE?

In order to determine who or what the bride of Christ may be, the first thing that needs to be established is if Jesus has a bride. Revelation 21:1–4 and 21:9–14 both state that Jesus has one. So does Rev 19:6–8a:

> 6 Then I heard what sounded like a great multitude, like the roar of rushing waters and like loud peals of thunder, shouting:
> "Hallelujah!
> For our Lord God Almighty reigns.
> 7 Let us rejoice and be glad
> and give him glory!
> For *the wedding of the Lamb has come,*
> and *his bride has made herself ready.*
> 8 Fine linen, bright and clean,
> was given her to wear."

John 3:28–29 also suggests that Jesus has a bride:

> 28 You yourselves can testify that I [John the baptist] said, "I am not the Messiah but am sent ahead of him." 29 The bride belongs to the bridegroom. *The friend who attends the bridegroom waits and listens for him, and is full of joy* when he hears the bridegroom's voice. That joy is mine and is now complete.

Although John 3:28–29 doesn't explicitly state that Jesus has a bride, it does compare John's relationship with Jesus as if Jesus has one. John understood that he was not Jesus' bride, however, and instead was a friend of the bridegroom.

Matthew 9:14–15 seems to indicate as well that Jesus has a bride:

> 14 Then John's disciples came and asked him, "How is it that we and the Pharisees fast, but your disciples do not fast?"
> 15 Jesus answered, *"How can the guests of the bridegroom mourn while he is with them?* The time will come when the bridegroom will be taken from them; then they will fast."

Matthew 9:14–15, like John 3:28–29, doesn't explicitly state that Jesus has a bride. But like the passage in John, it compares Jesus' relationship to his disciples as if Jesus has one. Jesus' disciples are described in Matt 9:14–15 as guests of the bridegroom, however, not as Jesus' bride.

Neither passage identifies who or what the bride of Christ may be.

IS THE CHURCH JESUS' BRIDE?

There are two passages in the New Testament that suggest that the church may be the bride of Christ. Both were written by Paul. Ephesians 5:25–28 is the passage most often cited to support that the church is Jesus' bride:

> 25 *Husbands, love your wives, just as Christ loved the church and gave himself up for her* 26 to make her holy, cleansing her by the washing with water through the word, 27 and to present her to himself as a radiant church, without stain or wrinkle or any other blemish, but holy and blameless. 28 In this same way, husbands ought to love their wives as their own bodies. He who loves his wife loves himself.

Second Corinthians 11:1–4 is the other passage sometimes cited to support the belief that the church is the bride of Christ:

> 1 I hope you will put up with me in a little foolishness. Yes, please put up with me! 2 I am jealous for you with a godly jealousy. *I promised you to one husband, to Christ*, so that I might present you as a pure virgin to him. 3 But I am afraid that just as Eve was deceived by the serpent's cunning, your minds may somehow be led astray from your sincere and pure devotion to Christ. 4 For if someone comes to you and preaches a Jesus other than the Jesus we preached, or if you receive a different spirit from the one you received, or a different gospel from the one you accepted, you put up with it easily enough.

Although both Eph 5:25–28 and 2 Cor 11:1–4 seem to describe Jesus as a husband and the church as his wife, neither passage explicitly states this is so. Paul, in Eph 5:25–28, was simply encouraging husbands to treat their wives sacrificially in the same way that Jesus treats those he loves. And though Paul did use the word "husband" in 2 Cor 11:2 to symbolize a Christian's relationship to Jesus, his purpose for doing so seems to have been to urge those who follow Jesus to remain faithful to Jesus and his message of salvation no matter what others promote or teach. This call for followers of Jesus to be faithful to Jesus is similar to God's call for wives to be faithful to their husbands.

Although neither Eph 5:25–28 nor 2 Cor 11:1–4 explicitly state that the church is the bride of Christ, that doesn't mean this association isn't valid. It could be true even if not explicitly stated. It does present a problem, however, if it is true. Consider, for example, these verses:

- "Now you are the body of Christ, and each one of you is a part of it" (1 Cor 12:27).
- 22 "And God placed all things under his feet and appointed him to be head over everything for the church, 23 which is his body, the fullness of him who fills everything in every way" (Eph 1:22–23).

The verses above explicitly state that the church is the body of Christ. But if the church is the body of Christ, how can it also be the bride of Christ? It seems to me that the church can't be both and must be one or the other.

In this case, I lean more towards the association that is explicitly stated than the one that is implied and have concluded that the church is the body of Christ, not the bride of Christ.

COULD ISRAEL BE JESUS' BRIDE?

There is a much stronger case that the people of Israel—the Jews—are the bride of Christ, as their relationship with God is often compared in Scripture to the relationship between a husband and wife. Here are five examples:

- 5 "'For *your Maker is your husband*—
  the Lord Almighty is his name—
  the Holy One of Israel is your Redeemer;
  he is called the God of all the earth.
  6 The Lord will call you back
    as if you were a wife deserted and distressed in spirit—
  a wife who married young,
    only to be rejected,' says your God" (Isa 54:5–6).

- 4 "No longer will they call you Deserted,
    or name your land Desolate.
  But you will be called Hephzibah [which means, 'my delight
      is in her'],
    and your land Beulah [which means, 'married'];
  for the Lord will take delight in you,
    and *your land will be married*.
  5 As a young man marries a young woman,
    so will your Builder marry you;
  as a bridegroom rejoices over his bride,
    so will your God rejoice over you" (Isa 62:4–5).

- "'Return, faithless people,' declares the Lord, 'for *I am your husband*. I will choose you—one from a town and two from a clan—and bring you to Zion'" (Jer 3:14).

- 31 "'The days are coming,' declares the Lord,
  'when I will make a new covenant

> with the people of Israel
> and with the people of Judah.
> 32 It will not be like the covenant
> I made with their ancestors
> when I took them by the hand
> to lead them out of Egypt,
> *because they broke my covenant,*
> *though I was a husband to them,*
> declares the Lord" (Jer 31:31–32).

- 19 "*I will betroth you to me forever*;
  I will betroth you in righteousness and justice,
  in love and compassion.
  20 I will betroth you in faithfulness,
  and you will acknowledge the Lord" (Hos 2:19–20).

These passages strongly suggest that God has a relationship with Israel that is comparable to the relationship between a husband and wife. Even though Israel often committed spiritual adultery by serving other gods, there is no indication in Scripture that God has divorced the nation of Israel or its people, or that he ever will. In this sense, God's relationship with Israel seems to be unbreakable.

This conclusion is supported by these verses in Jer 31:33–36:

> 33 "This is the covenant I will make with the people of Israel
> after that time," declares the Lord.
> "I will put my law in their minds
> and write it on their hearts.
> I will be their God,
> and they will be my people.
> 34 No longer will they teach their neighbor,
> or say to one another, 'Know the Lord,'
> because they will all know me,
> from the least of them to the greatest,"
> declares the Lord.
> "For I will forgive their wickedness
> and will remember their sins no more"
> 35 This is what the Lord says,
> he who appoints the sun
> to shine by day,
> who decrees the moon and stars
> to shine by night,

> who stirs up the sea
> so that its waves roar—
> the LORD Almighty is his name:
> 36 "Only if these decrees vanish from my sight,"
> declares the LORD,
> "will Israel ever cease
> being a nation before me."

God promised that he would always remain faithful to Israel, even if the people of Israel were unfaithful to him.

As God so aptly said through Hosea, "I will betroth you [Israel] to me forever" (Hos 2:19).

What, then, could be happening in Rev 19:7-8 when Jesus' bride is clothed in white linen and made ready for her bridegroom? What could be happening in Rev 21:2 when John sees "the Holy City, the new Jerusalem, coming down out of heaven from God, prepared as a bride beautifully dressed for her husband?"

One possibility is this image symbolizes the spiritual restoration of the Jews following centuries of living as if they don't need Jesus to be their Lord and messiah. This spiritual restoration may coincide with the day they say, "'Blessed is he who comes in the name of the Lord'" (Matt 23:39)—the day when God pours out "on the house of David and the inhabitants of Jerusalem a spirit of grace and supplication"—the day when "they . . . look on me, the one they have pierced, and . . . mourn for him as one mourns for an only child, and grieve bitterly for him as one grieves for a firstborn son" (Zech 12:10).

WHAT IS JESUS' RELATIONSHIP TO THE CHURCH?

If Israel and not the church is the bride of Christ, then what is the relationship of the church to Jesus and his bride? And what does this have to do with the rapture of the church?

I have found these two passages helpful when trying to make sense of this:

- 17 "If some of the branches have been broken off, and *you, though a wild olive shoot, have been grafted in among the others and now share in the nourishing sap from the olive root,* 18 do not consider yourself to be superior to those other branches. If you do, consider this: You do not support the root, but the root supports you. 19 You will say then,

'Branches were broken off so that I could be grafted in.' 20 Granted. But they were broken off because of unbelief, and you stand by faith. Do not be arrogant, but tremble. 21 For if God did not spare the natural branches, he will not spare you either" (Rom 11:17–21).

- 26 "So in Christ Jesus you are all children of God through faith, 27 for all of you who were baptized into Christ have clothed yourselves with Christ. 28 There is neither Jew nor Gentile, neither slave nor free, nor is there male and female, for you are all one in Christ Jesus. 29 *If you belong to Christ, then you are Abraham's seed*, and heirs according to the promise" (Gal 3:26–29).

Romans 11:17–21 states that Christians have been grafted onto an olive root. This olive root is typically understood to symbolize Israel and God's promise that he would bless the world through this nation—through Abraham and his descendants (Gen 12:3)—a promise fulfilled when Jesus' sacrificial death paid the penalty for everyone's sins. The natural branches of this olive tree are from Abraham's lineage. Gentile believers have been grafted onto it. Both sets of believers—Jew and gentile—are now connected to a tree that only the people of Israel were originally part of.

In Gal 3:26–29, Paul stated this relationship in a different way. Paul said that all who belong to Christ are part of Abraham's seed—that all Christians are, in some fashion, part of Israel.

What's apparent from these two passages is that there is an intimate connection between gentile and Jewish believers. Since they now share the same root, they are bonded together in a way that is difficult to break.

It seems to me that whatever happens to the original branches and those grafted in will occur *simultaneously*. Just like wheat and weeds, which won't be separated until the harvest, no separation between the natural branches and those grafted in later will occur prior to end of the age—prior to the moment when Jesus returns to judge the wicked and reward the righteous.

What is inarguable is that Jesus' bride doesn't appear to be united with him until nearly all the events described in Revelation have taken place (Rev 21:1–4). And instead of being taken up to heaven to be with Jesus, John described Jesus' bride as "coming down out of heaven from God" (Rev 21:2, 9).

THE PRE-WRATH RAPTURE

Another term similar to "pre-tribulation rapture," and sometimes considered synonymous with it, is "pre-wrath rapture."

What some believers seem to mean when they use the term "pre-wrath rapture" is that, at some point, God will be so fed up with mankind's rejection of him and the evils that result from this that he will remove from the earth all who are committed followers of Jesus so he can unleash his fury on those who have rejected him and his ways. This exercise of wrath and judgment will last seven years.

Some who believe in a pre-wrath rapture link their understanding of it to Rom 1:18–20:

> 18 *The wrath of God is being revealed from heaven against all the godlessness and wickedness of people*, who suppress the truth by their wickedness, 19 since what may be known about God is plain to them, because God has made it plain to them. 20 For since the creation of the world God's invisible qualities—his eternal power and divine nature—have been clearly seen, being understood from what has been made, so that people are without excuse.

Romans 1 continues by describing evils that many Christians find abhorrent. These include unnatural sexual relations (v. 26–27), as well as greed, depravity, envy, murder, strife, deceit, and malice (v. 29ab). But Romans 1 also lists issues that Christians sometimes find less objectionable. These include gossip, slander, arrogance, boasting, disobedience to parents, and lack of fidelity (vv. 29c–30).

It seems to me that Paul's purpose in listing these issues was not for Christians to focus on how angry God is over the multitudes of ways people sin, however, nor was it why God may be on the verge of expressing his wrath in such a decisive and dramatic fashion. I believe Paul listed these in order to magnify the extent of God's grace.

Romans 2:1–4 records what Paul wrote following the evils he described in Rom 1:18–32:

> 1 You, therefore, have no excuse, you who pass judgment on someone else, for at whatever point you judge another, you are condemning yourself, because *you who pass judgment do the same things*. 2 Now we know that God's judgment against those who do such things is based on truth. 3 So when you, a mere human being, pass judgment on them and yet do the same things, do you think you will escape God's judgment? 4 Or do you show contempt for

the riches of his kindness, forbearance and patience, not realizing that *God's kindness is intended to lead you to repentance.*

The verses highlighted above are more aligned with my understanding of how God responds to the myriad ways people live contrary to his will. They remind me that I do many of the things I often condemn others for (v. 1). They also remind me that it is God's kindness and not his wrath that leads people to repentance (v. 4).

There are other ways I have found the concept of a pre-wrath rapture to be inconsistent with my understanding of God's character. For example:

- It suggests that God has a desire to punish unbelievers and the unrighteous for an extended period of time before throwing them into a "blazing furnace" where there will be "weeping and gnashing of teeth" (Matt 13:42). I don't find this conclusion consistent with Peter's observation that God is "patient . . . not wanting anyone to perish, but [wanting] everyone to come to repentance" (2 Pet 3:9).

- There could be nothing worse than ending up in an eternal, blazing furnace. If this is so, then why would God precede this with an extended period of additional suffering when his goal is to redeem people, not punish them?

- It ignores Paul's assertion that Christians do many of the things they often condemn others for and are just as deserving of judgment (Rom 2:3).

The concept of a pre-wrath rapture is also inconsistent with what Jesus was teaching through the Parable of the Weeds: those who are followers of Jesus and those who are not will be living together in the same field until the harvest at the end of the age.

Chapter 11

The Other Parables

But the seed falling on good soil refers to someone who hears the word and understands it. This is the one who produces a crop, yielding a hundred, sixty or thirty times what was sown.

MATTHEW 13:23

BEFORE WRAPPING THIS UP, I want to return to Matt 13 where the Parable of the Weeds is recorded.

In chapter 3, when I discussed the five parables recorded in Matt 24 and 25, I noted how important it is when trying to understand parables grouped together to note what they have in common. This convention is useful when trying to understand the six parables in Matt 13 as well. That's because each of these six has something in common. Each of these parables focuses on an aspect of the kingdom of heaven.

But unlike the parables in Matt 24 and 25, which I contend are using different stories to communicate the same message, it seems to me that the parables in Matt 13 are adding something to a core message—a message found in the Parable of the Weeds. This message is that the wheat and weeds are going to be living alongside each other until the harvest at the end of the age. What the other parables in Matt 13 contribute to this message is what Christians are urged to do in light of it.

What follows are my thoughts about what the other parables in Matt 13 contribute to understanding the message Jesus was trying to convey through the Parable of the Weeds.

THE PARABLE OF THE SOWER

The first parable in Matt 13 is the Parable of the Sower (Matt 13:1–9):

> 1 That same day Jesus went out of the house and sat by the lake. 2 Such large crowds gathered around him that he got into a boat and sat in it, while all the people stood on the shore. 3 Then he told them many things in parables, saying: "A farmer went out to sow his seed. 4 As he was scattering the seed, some fell along the path, and the birds came and ate it up. 5 Some fell on rocky places, where it did not have much soil. It sprang up quickly, because the soil was shallow. 6 But when the sun came up, the plants were scorched, and they withered because they had no root. 7 Other seed fell among thorns, which grew up and choked the plants. 8 Still other seed fell on good soil, where it produced a crop—a hundred, sixty or thirty times what was sown. 9 *Whoever has ears, let them hear.*"

Matthew 13:18–23 records Jesus' explanation of this parable:

> 18 Listen then to what the Parable of the Sower means: 19 When anyone hears the message about the kingdom and does not understand it, the evil one comes and snatches away what was sown in their heart. This is the seed sown along the path. 20 The seed falling on rocky ground refers to someone who hears the word and at once receives it with joy. 21 But since they have no root, they last only a short time. *When trouble or persecution comes because of the word, they quickly fall away.* 22 The seed falling among the thorns refers to *someone who hears the word, but the worries of this life and the deceitfulness of wealth choke the word, making it unfruitful.* 23 But the seed falling on good soil refers to someone who hears the word and understands it. This is the one who produces a crop, yielding a hundred, sixty or thirty times what was sown.

There are two things I want to point out regarding the Parable of the Sower. The first is the phrase, "Whoever has ears, let them hear" (v. 9). This phrase seems to be used in Scripture when the speaker or writer wanted to emphasize the urgency of paying attention to what they had to say and taking some action in response to it. This phrase is used numerous times in Revelation, including in what John wrote to each of the seven churches in Asia (Rev 2–3). It also precedes John's warning that Satan's war against followers of Jesus would result in some Christians being taken captive and some killed (Rev 13:9–10).

The second thing I want to point out are the specific issues Jesus was addressing. Although the gospel message sometimes lands on ground where it doesn't grow at all (v. 19), sometimes it fails to bear fruit because of "trouble or persecution" (v. 21), and sometimes because of "the worries of life and the deceitfulness of wealth" (v. 22).

These issues are similar to the concerns Jesus had when he told his disciples about the challenging times that lay ahead for them (Matt 24:9–13). Jesus told his disciples that they were going to experience many troubles, including being persecuted for being followers of him. Jesus promised, however, that those who stood firm to the end—those who were perhaps like those in the Parable of the Sower who "hears the word and understands it" (Matt 13:23)—would be saved (Matt 24:13).

The Parable of the Sower provides a framework for understanding some of the challenges Christians will face as they wait for the kingdom of heaven to be established. This framework is fleshed out in subsequent chapters of Matthew as well as in other New Testament books, including Revelation, with an emphasis on how Christians are to respond when they face these challenges.

When will these challenges end? According to the Parable of the Weeds, not until the final separation of the righteous from the unrighteous at the end of the age.

THE PARABLE OF THE MUSTARD SEED AND THE PARABLE OF THE YEAST

Some may conclude from the Parable of the Sower that in order to be saved, one must remain faithful to Jesus throughout their life and must be fruitful as well. That would not be an unreasonable conclusion. It is also consistent with Jesus' promise, as well as warning, that those who stand firm to the end, and perhaps *only* those who stand firm to the end, will be saved (Matt 24:13). But how much faith is required to be saved? How much faith is needed to avoid experiencing the fate of seeds that do not bear fruit? How much faith must one have to stand firm to the end?

Based on the next two parables in Matt 13, I would argue, "Not much." The first is the Parable of the Mustard Seed (Matt 13:31–32):

> 31 He told them another parable: "The kingdom of heaven is like a mustard seed, which a man took and planted in his field.
> 32 Though *it is the smallest of all seeds, yet when it grows, it is the*

largest of garden plants and becomes a tree, so that the birds come and perch in its branches."

The second is the Parable of the Yeast (Matt 13:33):

> He told them still another parable: "The kingdom of heaven is like yeast that a woman took and mixed into about sixty pounds of flour until *it worked all through the dough*."

Some have tried to apply the Parable of the Mustard Seed to prayer, believing, for example, that if they have just a little faith, whatever they are praying for will be given to them. This belief seems to be based in part on how Jesus associated a mustard seed with faith in Matt 17:19–20:

> 19 Then the disciples came to Jesus in private and asked, "Why couldn't we drive it out?"
>
> 20 He replied, "Because you have so little faith. Truly I tell you, *if you have faith as small as a mustard seed*, you can say to this mountain, 'Move from here to there,' and it will move. Nothing will be impossible for you."

In the context of Matt 13, however, I don't believe the Parable of the Mustard seed has anything to do with the kingdom of earth and what prayers will or will not be answered as we live in that kingdom. It is my conclusion that the sole intent of this parable and the one that follows, the Parable of the Yeast, is to tell something about the kingdom of heaven and how much faith one must have to be considered part of it.

Although the mustard seed is one of the smallest seeds, it has the potential of growing into a large, fruitful tree. But to be fruit-bearing, it must be planted in good soil, must remain in that soil, and must receive proper care.

What it takes for this small seed to grow into a fruitful tree is a more specific example of what Jesus was trying to convey in these verses in the Parable of the Sower:

- "Still other *seed fell on good soil*, where it produced a crop—a hundred, sixty or thirty times what was sown" (Matt 13:8).
- "But the *seed falling on good soil* refers to someone who hears the word and understands it. This is the one who produces a crop, yielding a hundred, sixty or thirty times what was sown" (Matt 13:23).

The Parable of the Yeast conveys a similar message. Just like it doesn't take much yeast to affect all the dough one is using to bake bread, it doesn't take much faith to become a fruitful member of the kingdom of heaven.

I find that encouraging.

THE PARABLE OF THE HIDDEN TREASURE AND THE PARABLE OF THE PEARL

The next two parables in Matt 13 use different illustrations to communicate the same message. The first of these is the Parable of the Hidden Treasure (Matt 13:44):

> The kingdom of heaven is like treasure hidden in a field. When a man found it, he hid it again, and then in his joy went and sold all he had and bought that field.

The second is the Parable of the Pearl (Matt 13:45–46):

> 45 Again, the kingdom of heaven is like a merchant looking for fine pearls. 46 When he found one of great value, he went away and sold everything he had and bought it.

Jesus used the Parable of the Sower to emphasize the importance of not letting trouble, persecution, the worries of life, or wealth cause one to fall away from their faith or fail to become a fruitful member of God's kingdom. One implication of the Parable of the Weeds is this faith must be maintained throughout one's life. The Parable of the Mustard Seed and the Parable of the Yeast provide encouragement that it doesn't take much faith to do this.

What the Parable of the Hidden Treasure and the Parable of the Pearl contribute to this is the importance of making it a priority to obtain, exhibit, and hold onto the quality of faith required to be a fruitful member of God's kingdom.

John 15:1–8 notes another way that Jesus stated this:

> 1 *I am the true vine*, and my Father is the gardener. 2 He cuts off every branch in me that bears no fruit, while every branch that does bear fruit he prunes so that it will be even more fruitful. 3 You are already clean because of the word I have spoken to you. 4 *Remain in me*, as I also remain in you. No branch can bear fruit by itself; it must remain in the vine. Neither can you bear fruit unless you *remain in me*.

The Other Parables

> 5 I am the vine; you are the branches. If you *remain in me* and I in you, you will bear much fruit; apart from me you can do nothing. 6 If you do not *remain in me*, you are like a branch that is thrown away and withers; such branches are picked up, thrown into the fire and burned. 7 If you *remain in me* and my words remain in you, ask whatever you wish, and it will be done for you. 8 This is to my Father's glory, that you bear much fruit, showing yourselves to be my disciples.

One key phrase in John 15:1–8 is "remain in me." Jesus repeated it five times to emphasize the importance of having and staying in a personal relationship with him. A Christian cannot be fruitful—cannot bear fruit—unless they stay connected to Jesus.

THE PARABLE OF THE NET

The sixth parable in Matt 13 is the Parable of the Net (Matt 13:47–50):

> 47 Once again, the kingdom of heaven is like a net that was let down into the lake and caught all kinds of fish. 48 When it was full, the fishermen pulled it up on the shore. Then they sat down and collected the good fish in baskets, but threw the bad away. 49 This is how it will be at the end of the age. The angels will come and separate the wicked from the righteous 50 and throw them into the blazing furnace, where there will be weeping and gnashing of teeth.

The message Jesus was conveying through the Parable of the Net is nearly identical to the one he was communicating through the Parable of the Weeds. For example:

- The events described include a gathering of two groups, each with a different fate (vv. 30, 48).
- The gatherings that take place occur at the end of the age (vv. 39, 49).
- The ones that do the gathering and separation are angels (vv. 39, 49).
- The wicked are thrown into a blazing furnace (vv. 41–42, 49–50).
- The righteous are spared (vv. 43, 48).

One reason Jesus may have repeated the message of the Parable of the Weeds using a different illustration was to reinforce what he told his disciples earlier: that no separation of the righteous from the unrighteous was going to take place until the harvest at the end of the age.

That was something they and other followers of Jesus would need to keep in mind as they faced the troubles, persecution, worries of life, and deceitfulness of wealth that lay ahead.

Some Final Thoughts

*Remember the law of my servant Moses,
the decrees and laws I gave him at Horeb for all Israel.*

MALACHI 4:4

As I reflect on what I've presented in this book, I am reminded of Mal 4:1–6:

> 1 "Surely *the day is coming; it will burn like a furnace.* All the arrogant and *every evildoer will be stubble, and the day that is coming will set them on fire,*" says the LORD Almighty. "Not a root or a branch will be left to them. 2 But for you who revere my name, the sun of righteousness will rise with healing in its rays. And you will go out and frolic like well-fed calves. 3 Then you will trample on the wicked; they will be ashes under the soles of your feet on the day when I act," says the LORD Almighty.
>
> 4 "*Remember the law of my servant Moses,* the decrees and laws I gave him at Horeb for all Israel.
>
> 5 "See, *I will send the prophet Elijah to you* before that great and dreadful day of the LORD comes. 6 He will turn the hearts of the parents to their children, and the hearts of the children to their parents; or else I will come and strike the land with total destruction."

God gave these prophecies to Malachi around 430 BC, over one hundred years after the Jews started returning to Israel following their exile in Babylon. One of God's goals when he spoke through Malachi was to voice his complaints regarding how his chosen people—the Jews—were living. But God addressed one of the Jews' burning concerns as well. They wanted to know when God was going to judge the wicked.

God told the Jews that there would be a day when "every evildoer will be stubble"—a day that "will set them on fire" (Mal 4:1). That day was not coming soon, however, at least not from their perspective. It would not come until someone walking in the footsteps of Elijah came as a messenger, preparing the way for the Lord (Mal 3:1, 4:5). This prophecy wasn't going to be fulfilled for nearly four hundred years—not until John the Baptist was identified by Jesus as the messenger Malachi was referring to (Matt 11:7–15).

The Jews in Malachi's day didn't know how long it would be before the prophecies recorded in Mal 4 were going to be fulfilled, of course. But they did know what God wanted them to do as they waited for them to be fulfilled. They were to "remember the law of my servant Moses, the decrees and laws I gave him at Horeb for all Israel" (Mal 4:4). In short, they were to be obedient to God.

This needs to be our focus as well as we consider the events the Bible says will characterize the end times. No matter when Jesus returns or under what circumstances he does so, God wants us to always be found doing what is commendable in his eyes.

Here are some other things I've learned as I consider what I've discussed in this book:

- Although this world is often a difficult place to live in, I should not allow that to be a source of distress, anxiety, or discouragement. There is a better world in my future, and that is something I can look forward to.
- Instead of hoping or believing I won't be subjected to trials, I should prepare for them as if they are inevitable.
- I need to do a better job living in ways that honor God in the imperfect world I'm in rather than longing so much for the perfect world that is to come.
- It's crucial that I not compromise my faith when faced with threats to my physical or financial well-bring for being a follower of Jesus.
- No matter how tough times may be, I can be confident that all will end well for me as long as I remain faithful to Jesus.
- If reaching the lost is so important to God that he sends an angel to preach the gospel to the entire world before the end comes (Rev 14:6–7), maybe I should be more involved in doing that as well.

Some Final Thoughts

- I shouldn't be in such a hurry for Jesus to return. For though Jesus' return will result in good things for me, it will result in terrible things for those unprepared for his return.

I hope you find the above relevant as well.

And so, if you have already packed your bags and are waiting for Jesus to whisk you away from this world so that you can be spared from the trials that lay ahead, my advice to you is this: *unpack those bags*! For if my understanding of the message Jesus was conveying through the Parable of the Weeds is correct—if we're going to be in this world for the duration of nearly all the terrible events the Bible says will characterize the end times—then we may need every piece of clothing in our spiritual closets to endure the troubles that lay ahead and remain faithful to Jesus in the midst of them.

Bibliography

Amazing Sanctuary. "The 2300 Days." https://www.amazingsanctuary.com/the-messiah/the-2300-days.

Bible Gateway. "Simon Maccabeus." Bible Gateway: Encyclopedia of the Bible. https://www.biblegateway.com/resources/encyclopedia-of-the-bible/Simon-Maccabeus.

Brice, William Charles, and Kathleen Mary Kenyon. "The Hasmonean Priest-Princes." Encyclopaedia Britannica, Sept. 9, 2025. https://www.britannica.com/place/Palestine/The-Hasmonean-priest-princes#ref478850.

Encyclopaedia Britannica. "Transitive Law." Nov. 4, 2016. https://www.britannica.com/topic/transitive-law.

History. "Masada." May 28, 2025. https://www.history.com/articles/masada.

Jimenez, Larry. "10 Things Believed to Be the Mark of the Beast." ListVerse, Aug. 26, 2024. https://listverse.com/2024/08/26/10-things-believed-to-be-the-mark-of-the-beast/.

Livius. "Titus' Siege of Jerusalem." Oct. 10, 2020. https://www.livius.org/articles/concept/roman-jewish-wars/roman-jewish-wars-4/.

Lohnes, Kate. "Siege of Jerusalem." Encyclopaedia Britannica, Aug. 29, 2018. https://www.britannica.com/event/Siege-of-Jerusalem-70.

Ludlow, Jared W. "The First Jewish Revolt Against Rome." In *New Testament History, Culture, and Society*, edited by Lincoln H. Blumell, 230–44. Salt Lake City: BYU Religious Studies Center, 2019. https://rsc.byu.edu/new-testament-history-culture-society/first-jewish-revolt-against-rome.

Miller, Tim. "The Fall of Jerusalem in 70 CE: A Story of Roman Revenge." Warfare History Network, July 2018. https://warfarehistorynetwork.com/article/the-fall-of-jerusalem-in-70-ce-a-story-of-roman-revenge/.

Milligan, Mark. "The Siege of Masada." Heritage Daily, Feb. 1, 2021. https://www.heritagedaily.com/2021/02/the-siege-of-masada.

Oates, Harry. "The Great Jewish Revolt of 66 CE." World History Encyclopedia, Aug. 28, 2015. https://www.worldhistory.org/article/823/the-great-jewish-revolt-of-66-ce/.

Pareles, Mo. "Cannibal Maria in the Siege of Jerusalem: New Approaches." Religion Compass, Nov. 30, 2023. https://compass.onlinelibrary.wiley.com/doi/10.1111/rec3.12479.

Perry, Tyler. "The Siege of Jerusalem in 70 CE." World History Encyclopedia, May 2, 2022. https://www.worldhistory.org/article/1993/the-siege-of-jerusalem-in-70-ce/.

Christian History Institute. "#103 Polycarp's Martyrdom." https://christianhistoryinstitute.org/study/module/polycarp.

Bibliography

Shea, William H. "When Did the Seventy Weeks of Daniel 9:24 Begin?" *Journal of the Adventist Theological Society* 2.1 (1991) 115–38. https://www.atsjats.org/when-did-the-seventy-weeks-of-daniel-924-begin.pdf.

www.ingramcontent.com/pod-product-compliance
Lightning Source LLC
Chambersburg PA
CBHW071211160426
43196CB00011B/2260